Common Courage

Common Courage

Daniel D. Kinley

VANTAGE PRESS INC.
New York

Cover design by Victor Mingovits
Painting by Don Troiani,
www.historical.imagebank.com

Vantage Press and the Vantage Press colophon
are registered trademarks of Vantage Press, Inc.

FIRST EDITION

All rights reserved, including the right of
reproduction in whole or in part in any form.

Copyright © 2012 by Daniel D. Kinley

Published by Vantage Press, Inc.
419 Park Ave. South, New York, NY 10016

Manufactured in the United States of America
ISBN: 978-0533-165032

Library of Congress Catalog Card No: 2011911086

0 9 8 7 6 5 4 3 2 1

DEDICATION

This book is dedicated to my father, Daniel Dalton Kinley, who obviously suffered from the separation and divorce of his parents when he was a young boy. Apparently his father did not honor the commitment to his wife and family.

My father never mentioned the trying events to me but the experience left its mark on him. After his mother remarried, he legally changed his name from Percival to his stepfather's name of Kinley.

My father died in 1996 and will never know the details of the historic events his great-great-great-great grandfather experienced that are described in this book. Nor will he get a chance to re-evaluate his feelings about his given name of Percival.

CONTENTS

Preface   ix

Chapter 1
Bloody Initiation   1

Chapter 2
Waste of War   21

Chapter 3
War's Pendulum   35

Chapter 4
Hopeful Finish   55

Chapter 5
War Returns   77

Chapter 6
Longest Campaign   99

Epilogue   123

Maps   129

Appendix A: Muster lists of the military companies in which Timothy Percival served during the French and Indian War   135

Appendix B: August 27, 1776, Seventeenth Continental Regiment Casualty List, Battle of Long Island   139

Bibliography   143

Endnotes   151

PREFACE

This book began in 2005 with a copy of my uncle's application to the National Society, Sons of the American Revolution, tracing our lineage to Timothy Percival. In what turned out to be a naïve thought, I decided it would be interesting to discover a little about the man, Timothy Percival, and in what way he served during the War for Independence. It became clear after a little research that Timothy took part in a number of defining moments in eighteenth-century American history, among them the French and Indian War. The scope of my study then ballooned from a minor research project intended to be shared with family members, to a major effort to bring his experiences to life.

I never imagined one could find delight in scouring old property and church records, or staring for hours at microfilm records of the scribbles made by military clerks on campaigns conducted 250 years ago. I don't think my eyes will ever forgive me, but the unraveling of the mystery of Timothy Percival's life has been an enjoyable experience. It has led me to numerous museums, archives, and historical sites, where staff members fight a struggle against great odds to preserve history and present it to the public in a meaningful way. Their efforts have been worthwhile for me. I cannot fully describe the feeling of holding a 250-year-old document containing my relative's name. Suffice it to say, it was very meaningful indeed.

Pulling together this voluminous research, I have attempted to bring to life the actions and events surrounding a particular and largely unknown individual within a generally well-known and broad historical time period. To do so required research into a variety of material, from the specifics of Timothy Percival's personal life, to descriptions and retellings of our shared, and presumably well known, major historical events. Particularly challenging has been the fact that I have uncovered no primary sources in Timothy Percival's own hand or even directly about him. Therefore, in recording Timothy's life, I have had to make a number of logical assumptions, the biggest being that unless I found a record stating otherwise, I assumed he was with the men of his company, or regiment, throughout each campaign. In this way I could use the written journals and diaries of others in the same military unit or particular campaign to visualize Timothy's experience. Again, lacking any written material from Timothy, this was my only recourse.

Many of the particulars of Timothy's life were gleaned from detailed documents such as Homer Brainard's record of the descendants of James Percival; state historical collections such as Rolls of Connecticut Men in the French and Indian War, 1755–1762, and Record of Service of Connecticut Men in the War of Revolution; as well as numerous other public records, including census, tax, and land and property records. As these documents may be new to the general follower of colonial history, I have noted them throughout the story.

I have also interjected my twenty-five years of personal experiences as a historical re-enactor to help describe Timothy's military life. I have slept in a canvas tent in a military camp with thousands of other re-enactors, trudged through the mud wearing replica shoes from the period, and cleaned the rust from my musket resulting from only a simple morning dew. The musket drills of the period have been imprinted in my brain by shouting drillmasters looking for the slightest fault in my actions. Foul-tasting black powder has lodged between my teeth as I have struggled to load and fire my musket while facing an imposing bayonet charge by hundreds of redcoats. I have also learned to fear the wild yelps and hoots of Native American re-enactors scurrying through the forest to attack one's flank. While I have never had to experience real combat, through re-enacting I know how fortunate I am to have missed it. I have incredibly deep respect for those who actually fought these many battles of the past.

To help provide a description of the environments in which Timothy lived, I traveled to East Haddam, Connecticut, and the area of Kentucky where Timothy is probably buried. I have hiked and canoed in the area of the Adirondacks in New York where Timothy served on a number of campaigns, and I have visited many of the battle sites where he experienced the horror of war. I was also fortunate to represent Timothy at the 250th anniversary of the Battle of Lake George in September 2005, where I helped "defend" the English camp in the approximate place where Timothy would have been on September 8, 1755.

As for the major events described in this story—the French and Indian War, and the War of Independence—there are many excellent sources that the reader can consult. These can be found in the bibliography. Because these events are generally well known and well described by others, I have not referenced them as I have cited the diaries, journals, and other primary sources.

Timothy's story is, in effect, the story of thousands of men—those living in New England during the tumultuous latter half of the eighteenth century. They were not trained soldiers, rather simple struggling farmers who mustered their bravery to repeatedly volunteer for the arduous military campaigns of the period. Gaining experience in the French and Indian War, they then went on to form a critical core of veteran officers in the struggle for American independence, often alongside or leading their own sons. The many months of separation from their families and farms were a sure strain on both their personal lives and economic livelihoods. And the shared perils and fears they encountered preparing for and engaged in battle were unimaginable, though perhaps often bonding. This is indeed a story of common courage.

Common Courage

CHAPTER 1

Bloody Initiation

It was a time of wonder and a time of worry. At the dawn of 1755, Timothy Percival was a man with few immediate prospects. He was the second son of John and Hannah Percival in a family of nine brothers and sisters, with a tenth child expected in the summer. His father was only forty-nine years old, so it could be a long time before the division of his landholdings among the heirs.[1] The farmland in the northwest corner of East Haddam, where Timothy grew up, was typical of the Colony of Connecticut. The earth contained more than its fair share of boulders, and forced the inhabitants to scratch a living out of the ground. Every spring more rocks would appear in the fields, having been raised from the earth by winter frosts. The Percivals labored to remove these impediments to the plow and, probably, cursed the mischief as the work of the devil, who some believed pushed the stones up from hell to torment the settlers and test their good Christian souls. Just as

Job and Jesus had their faith and patience tested in the scriptures, so too did New England farmers shoulder their burdens and persevere.

The struggle with the land drove the Percivals to find other means to augment their income. Timothy's father used his blacksmith skills to aid the people of both East Haddam and Middletown, the neighboring town to the north, producing shoes for horses and cattle, nails, and all kinds of ironwork. The Percivals were somewhat skilled as weavers and leather shoemakers as well. In addition, they grew grain and flax.[2] The flax could be molded into linen, and the wool from their sheep spun into thread. Taken together, their numerous talents and committed labor established a successful family farm.

The realities of colonial life and changed conditions over time had modified the character of the New England colonists. They were still largely English yeomen, of Puritan origin, but the confines of the narrow village life, the persistent need to pursue economic gain, and the rigorous disciplines of Puritanism had generally produced a different breed. Their ownership of the family farm that fed and clothed them provided an independence and control over their own destiny not experienced by the populace of the mother country. Their governments, originally theocratic in form, now leaned democratic. While certain families maintained prominence, there were no clear class divisions. Popular power was widely enjoyed across varied economic means, as was popular education. And examples of public and private virtue abounded.[3]

The Percival family seemed somewhat typical in this respect. They struggled nobly for economic leverage against the harsh temporal realities of their place and time. Moreover, they proved over and over again to have a keen sense of civic virtue, making them willing to sacrifice personal comforts for broader and, over time, increasingly nationalistic causes.

In August 1754, Timothy married Mary Fuller, a beautiful bride with blue eyes and black hair; beyond lovely, she was known to be bright, witty, and fun. She was a descendant of Edward Fuller, who had braved the crossing of the Atlantic in a tiny ship named the Mayflower to establish the Massachusetts Bay Colony.[4] All told, Mary was a good choice as partner for the hard enterprise of raising a New England family of their own.

The two had enjoyed their new life together for only seven months when faced with a grave decision. The Connecticut Assembly resolved in March of 1755 to raise a military force to join with the colonies of Massachusetts, New Hampshire, Rhode Island, and New York in an expedition to counter the encroachments of the French onto English territory. Serving as a provincial soldier on this expedition would earn cash, which would be very helpful in starting a family, but it would mean months of separation for Timothy and Mary. There was the very real possibility of death or maiming for Timothy as well. Ten years before, during the last war with France, thousands of New Englanders had joined in an expedition against the French fortress town of Louisbourg. The part-time provincial soldiers conducted a siege of this fortress (which guarded the important sea route to the Saint Lawrence River in Canada) and captured it. That amazing success inspired the colonists in 1755 to join in the current adventure. Timothy had to decide whether earning extra money was worth the risk.

Timothy's father was an officer in the local North Company Militia of East Haddam[5] so the question of serving in the present conflict was pondered by the whole family. Yet service in the town militia required only a few days of drill per year, and even if the Connecticut Assembly activated the militia, it would only be for short periods of emergency. The coming war would require service of many months away from the family farm. John, his older brother, and James, his younger brother, whose nineteenth birthday was approaching in July, were all old enough to serve. Rowland, thirteen; Francis, eleven; Gurdon, five; and Paul, three,[6] were too young to be considered. Yet every member of the family, both young and old, had chores to complete. The children were taught to be efficient with the use of their time; that industry was a virtue, and laziness the worst form of sin. Hence they should rise early and be useful before school and be home promptly to do chores in the evening. Their time at home should involve some service to the family—such as bringing in wood for the fire, providing food and water for the livestock, picking berries, gathering vegetables, spooling the yarn, and performing all errands.[7] If any one of them served in the military, the others would have to pick up the slack. After all the aspects of the situation were discussed, they reached the decision that only Timothy, twenty-one years of age, would volunteer.

All of the northern English Colonies had trouble raising enough volunteers for their provincial regiments, but the Colony of New York experienced the biggest delay. Connecticut was able to attract men faster, so New York asked for help. In May, the Connecticut Assembly authorized the raising of three companies of men, each one-hundred strong, to serve the Colony of New York. Eliezer Fitch was appointed to the rank of major to command these three companies, and Samuel Dimock of Saybrook, Connecticut, was appointed captain of one of the companies.[8] Captain Dimock was fifty-three years old and an experienced commander. He had been a sea captain and captain of provincial troops in the previous war with France.[9] Timothy, along with Gershom Rowley, who grew up in the same neighborhood of East Haddam, joined Dimock's company on June 9.[10] Timothy could look forward to earning twenty-eight shillings per month in the army,[11] money he desperately needed (one valuable cow alone cost about seventy shillings).[12] Still, though economically promising, saying goodbye to his family, especially to Mary, was undoubtedly painful.

The plan of action for the 1755 campaign season was ambitious, including four thrusts against the French. Major-General Edward Braddock, a regular British army officer, would lead an army of British regulars and provincial troops from Virginia, across the Appalachian Mountains, and attack the French Fort Duquesne, located at present-day Pittsburgh, Pennsylvania. General William Shirley, governor of the Massachusetts Bay Colony, would take a force from Albany, New

York, and move west to Lake Ontario. General William Johnson, from New York, was given the task of leading another army from Albany and advancing north to wrest control of southern Lake Champlain from the French. Meanwhile, Colonel Robert Monckton, another regular British officer, who was stationed in present-day Nova Scotia (called Acadia by the French inhabitants) would consolidate English control of that province.

Timothy was appointed to the rank of corporal in Dimock's company.[13] The military ranks descended from general, passed through colonel, major, captain, lieutenant, ensign, sergeant, and corporal, and ended with the common soldier, called a private, or sentinel. Timothy's rank of corporal meant that the soldiers in his company would look to him to solve their problems and frustrations with military life. Timothy's company was assigned to the army of General Johnson.

In early summer the area around Albany, New York, became overrun with English soldiers. Both General Shirley and General Johnson had determined to assemble their armies there to start their respective campaigns. Timothy considered this town to be the frontier area of the English colonies and thus found his military experience from the onset to be very different from his existence in East Haddam. To the west lived the Indians of the Iroquois Confederacy: the Mohawk, Oneidas, Onondagas, Cayugas, and Senecas. To the north lived the Abenakis, a tribe allied to the French and frequent raiders of the English settlements in New England. To the east were the mountains and wilderness of western Massachusetts. To the south flowed the Hudson River, the main line of communication and trade with New York harbor. The brick-and-stone architecture of Albany was also very different from the wood clapboard buildings of New England. The houses were tall and narrow, some with stair-like gables crowning their facades. The predominately Dutch settlers of Albany were successful traders with the Indians, and even the French, so this conflict was viewed as an interruption to their trade. Timothy and the thousands of other English soldiers camped around Albany were considered by the Dutch as a foreign army. Both the expeditions of Shirley and Johnson did provide a financial boost to the Dutch traders though, as the English armies competed for food, supplies, boats, and skilled laborers.

Still, both campaigns were delayed, precisely due to shortages and rising prices for necessities. The provincial soldiers had volunteered for one campaign season and were therefore eager to advance against the French stationed in Fort St. Frederic at Crown Point, controlling southern Lake Champlain. In the past the French had used this fort as a base to supply the dreaded Indian raiders as they moved south to attack the English settlements. St. Frederic was more than a French outpost to the New Englanders; it represented aid to the hated Indian war parties that ravaged the frontier, burning farms and killing or capturing members of the frontier families. Upon capturing this fort, the provincial soldiers hoped to return home as quickly as possible. Needless to say, the delays in Albany tried the patience of the men, among them those in Timothy's company, who could do nothing to change their situation.

A lack of supplies was not the sole problem. Colonial political leaders created further delays as they squabbled over the ranks of their respective officers. Connecticut politicians refused to let their leading officer, Phineas Lyman, serve under General Johnson unless Lyman had the same rank.[14] As a result, Lyman was eventually appointed a general as well. It seems the politicians were as concerned with fame and fortune as with the stated goal of defeating the French. Meanwhile, the summer advanced while the colonial troops still waited near Albany.

Finally the provincial units were ordered north to cut a wagon road through the forests in an area called the Great Carrying Place. This was a fourteen-mile stretch of land between the point where the Hudson River bends south (after flowing east out of the Adirondack Mountains) and the southern end of Lake George. This strategic piece of wilderness linked the important water route of the Hudson River with the Lake

Champlain-Richelieu River route to the Saint Lawrence River in French Canada. The soldiers began construction of Fort Edward along the Hudson and continued building a road to Lake George, called Lake St. Sacrament by the French. This area had to be secured before the soldiers could advance further north to Crown Point. In many places a woodland path had to be widened into a road. Not only did the trees need to be cut, but the roots also had to be extracted or the resulting stumps leveled close to the ground. Rocks and other obstructions had to be dug out with hand tools, and bridges were constructed over streams. Swarms of biting insects tormented the men, making each day's labor all the longer and more strenuous.

Johnson, with the last contingent of his army, did not leave Albany until August 8. With the summer so far advanced, many men wondered if they would accomplish anything before the end of the season. Further, supplies for the men in Johnson's army were not consistently delivered. The shortages left the men without enough food at times. Many provisions were left behind because some civilian wagon owners, contracted to deliver the supplies, mutinied for lack of pay.[15] The situation was so dire it was suggested that a request for private funds from the public would be needed to purchase provisions.[16]

Through the hot and humid summer the men in Dimock's company and others from all the northern colonies had numerous duties. The roadwork continued, and Fort Edward needed to be finished. Wood-cutting parties constantly traveled into the forest to cut down the trees, trim off the branches, and drag the trunks to whichever project needed lumber or back to camp for firewood. The construction crews and supply wagons all had to be guarded from lurking enemy Indians ready to kill and scalp the less vigilant. Patrols were sent into the dark forests and onto the lakes in small boats or canoes to find the enemy. This wilderness was full of towering trees that blocked the sunlight. The resulting dim shade hid equally wild animals and enemy Indians waiting in ambush.

Timothy would also have to spend time practicing military drills that controlled how the soldiers would move, fire, and load as a group. The drills should have been performed every day for the men to become proficient, but all the other duties often prevented the soldiers from completing this task. One common drill alone had thirty-six motions which were easy to forget without daily practice. Drill was not popular either. It was boring and involved motions such as "poise your firelock," where Timothy and the other soldiers would have held their heavy muskets straight up in the air in front of their faces with only their right hands. It would take only moments before one's arm muscles would start to shake or cramp from the effort.[17] They also endeavored to remember the commands and actions needed to move units in the field from a marching column into battle line. As a corporal, Timothy was responsible for seeing that the men in the company performed the drill as ordered.

General Johnson also conducted special training exercises with the allied Mohawk Indians who would in turn conduct mock attacks on the English soldiers to accustom them to their way of fighting.[18] The Indians would spread out in the woods, using all available trees and rocks to hide their movements and protect themselves from enemy fire. The provincial soldiers easily saw the sensibleness of the tactic. At that juncture, approximately three hundred Mohawk warriors had joined Johnson's army to fight the French. They were led by the old Chief Hendrick, a friend of General Johnson.[19] To the soldiers, the Mohawks were both terrifying and fascinating in appearance. They usually shaved the hair on their heads except for a tuft on the top, and painted their faces red and black. Their nearly naked bodies were decorated with geometrically designed tattoos, and their noses and ears were adorned with silver rings. Much of their limited clothing, whether of buckskin or cloth, was festooned with elaborate beadwork. Some had even opened and stretched their earlobes so they hung like rope.[20]

By August, everyone in the army had heard the terrible news of the defeat of General Braddock's column advancing west from Virginia. The stories of enemy Indians scalping and torturing many of the fleeing English in Braddock's army lent a sobering tension to those on the Crown Point expedition. Fear became more prevalent as enemy Indians attacked parties of wood gatherers near the English camps in the Great Carrying Place. Reports of possible enemy Indian sightings increased. Keeping the men in Dimock's company calm surely became much more challenging.

The French were well informed of General Johnson's progress through their Indian scouts; they had even gained access to his plans and intentions from papers found in General Braddock's captured baggage. Baron Ludwig Dieskau, the French commander in North America, altered his plans after studying this information. He concentrated a force of over three thousand men consisting of regular troops, militia, and Indians to counter General Johnson's army. After leaving a few men to guard Crown Point, Dieskau pushed south with his army to Ticonderoga, a strategic peninsula guarding both Lake Champlain and the access from Lake George to Lake Champlain. The baron proceeded to fortify that important location. Scouts informed Dieskau of the English construction of Fort Edward, and he determined that it should be attacked before the English could complete it. He quickly moved south with a force of two hundred sixty elite regulars known as grenadiers, eight hundred French militia, and seven hundred Indians. Dieskau knew the English under Johnson outnumbered his force, but he was clearly waging his bets that his grenadiers could overpower any of the relatively untrained provincial militia in the English army.[21]

When Johnson's scouts learned of the French concentration at Ticonderoga, Johnson determined that he did not have enough men to advance against the French. He sent off letters to the colonial governments asking for more soldiers and deployed his army to defend the Great Carrying Place. About five hundred men from New Hampshire and New York were left to finish building and to defend Fort Edward, while Johnson advanced the rest of his army north to Lake George. A heavy rain soaked the army on September 3, making for an ever more miserable march. Some of the troops from Massachusetts arrived late to the Lake George camp and tried to sleep on the wet ground without tents to cover them. And an overall lack of logistical discipline in the command of the army caused the ranks more suffering. All told, it took quite a while for Timothy and the other soldiers to clear trees, pitch tents, and build storehouses for supplies at Lake George. By September 7 the camp had been organized, a site had been chosen upon which to build a fort, and the construction of boats had begun. Timothy, like most of the provincial soldiers, employed the woodworking and blacksmithing skills he had acquired at home to aid the army.

Dieskau's French force advanced south from Ticonderoga by way of Wood Creek, just to the east of Johnson's army, and by September 7 camped within a few miles of Fort Edward. Dieskau hoped to attack the fort the next day, but that night his Indian allies decided they would not attack the English on land they believed belonged to the English, determining that they would rather attack the English camped at Lake George because they believed that land belonged to the French.[22] It is possible the real reason for the Indians' proposal was that they preferred to avoid attacking fortifications whenever possible. Many of the French militia agreed with the Indians' proposal. Therefore, in order to keep his force together, Dieskau finally adopted the plan to attack the camp at Lake George.

Throughout September 7, reports of French and Indians in the area came to Johnson's army. The nerves of the provincial soldiers were strained as rumors swept through the camp like a wildfire. Sleep did not come easily for many that night. Early on the morning of September 8, Johnson held a council with his officers and Mohawk leaders. Johnson suggested a number of movements of men, of varying strengths, to find the French and aid Fort Edward. During this council the Mohawk leaders, under Chief Hendrick, voiced their apprehension about the proposals and, like his counterpart in the French force, Johnson altered his plans, deciding to send a force that morning to the aid of Fort Edward. This group consisted of two hundred fifty Mohawks, commanded by Hendrick, followed by Colonel Ephraim Williams, of Massachusetts, in overall command of the force, with five hundred provincials. Connecticut's Lieutenant-Colonel Nathan Whiting, second in command of this force, followed with another five hundred men. This force represented about a third of the three thousand men camped at Lake George and comprised a mix of men from different colonies, though it did not include Timothy's company.[23]

The French marched north on the morning of September 8 toward Lake George on the road recently cut through the wilderness by the English. As the French approached Lake George they entered a valley between French Mountain to the east and West Mountain to the west. This area was covered with dense forest, rocks, and thickets. To the east of the road, in a small gorge, flowed a small brook. The French scouts captured an Englishman who informed them of the approaching enemy column. Dieskau quickly prepared an ambush. He placed his regular troops to block the road and hid the militia and Indians in front, on either side of the road. Thus by the time the English column met the regulars, they would find the enemy on three sides of their column. The plan worked very well. The English, believing the French were close to Fort Edward, had not sent forward scouts at this point, and literally walked into the trap. Colonel Williams at once rallied his troops and tried to form them into a line, but he was struck down and died. Hendrick was also killed early in the fight. Whiting realized the horrible position his men faced, and ordered a retreat back to the lake. While retreating, Whiting continually turned his men and faced them toward the advancing French, each volley of their muskets bringing casualties to the French and gaining time for the English. By repeating this action with frequency, Whiting masterfully prevented the retreat to Lake George from becoming a rout.

After the force under Colonel Williams had marched out that morning with flags flying and drums beating, the remaining army prepared the defense of the camp. Axes were issued to details of men who were ordered to cut wood to be used to form a line of cover called breastworks. Wagons and even boats were placed in the breastworks to form a defensive line. The thud of axes hitting wood became so constant that it rumbled along the lakeside and echoed off the mountains. Timothy and others could likewise hear the musket fire from the ambush, and stopped working for a moment to better determine from which direction the new sound approached. Already worried about the reports of the French near Fort Edward, the provincials now faced the prospect that they were in fact much closer. As the musket fire ebbed and flowed it was quickly determined that the fighting was getting closer to Lake George. The officers screamed orders and the men dropped their tools. The soldiers scurried for their muskets and ammunition. They hastily formed into their companies and regiments. Johnson dispatched about three hundred men under Lieutenant Colonel Cole, from Rhode Island, to aid those withdrawing from the ambush and ordered the rest of the army to take positions to defend their camp.

The area was bordered by swamp to the west, the lake to the north, and woods everywhere else. The breastworks faced the woods to the south and east. Three cannon were hauled up to the defense line near where the road entered the camp; another was placed on the eastern end of the barricade. Timothy's company formed up behind the breastworks near the center and waited as many of those ambushed in the morning came back into camp, assisting their wounded comrades. These poor fellows with bloodied wounds and shattered limbs entered camp through the barricade, adding to the fear and confusion. Many probably recalled the myriad stories of death and torture inflicted on Braddock's defeated army earlier that summer and likely imagined it was recurring.

The men of Timothy's company had loaded their muskets with powder and ball and primed them with black powder from their powder horns in anticipation of the French attack. As they waited anxiously by the barricade, Timothy most likely tried to calm himself as well as the men around him.

The nervous provincials probably fidgeted with their muskets to check if they were properly primed and to make sure their flints were securely fastened. Most of them had never been in battle before and must have held secret doubts of their own fortitude.

Finally the remains of Whiting's command and Cole's relief forces returned. Many of the sweat-soaked men collapsed from exhaustion in the camp, but they were not able to rest peacefully. They were soon ordered to take positions behind the breastworks with the rest of the army. Soon the frightening war whoops of the pursuing Indians filled the air as they approached Johnson's army. The woods appeared alive and extremely menacing as the Indians and French militia spread out among the trees facing Timothy. Men caught in the ambush, or the bloody morning scout, as it was called, spread tales of bloodthirsty Indians carving pieces of hair and scalp off the heads of wounded comrades, often giving the impression that the English army was greatly outnumbered and adding to the trepidation felt by the rest of the defenders. Colonial officers struggled to keep their troops on the breastworks. Many of those whom fear consumed ran or tried to sneak to the rear, and the officers had to use threats of bodily harm to return them to the line.

Yet the French were almost as disordered from pursuit as the English were from retreat. Many of the Indians had spread out in the forest searching for scalps of fallen enemies, useful equipment left behind, and prisoners they could take home to incorporate into their tribe or sell to the French. Dieskau advanced toward the English with a much-reduced force, but he counted on his grenadiers to lead the way and to inspire the rest to follow the attack. With more whoops from the Indians, the grenadiers marched in perfect formation from the trees in their bright white coats with their deadly bayonets fixed to their muskets. All in a moment, the world must have seemed to explode around Timothy. Their musket and cannon fire were answered by the enemy, and the air was filled with lead. The grenadiers advanced valiantly and fired with precision, but the volume of bullets and well-directed cannon fire from the defenders drove them back. The proud grenadiers continued to attack numerous times but each time fell back, again into the woods. The French militia and Indians did not dare follow the grenadiers, yet they kept a constant fire on the English from cover in the forest.[24]

For what seemed an eternity, musket fire erupted along the lines of the opposing forces. Timothy would have heard the whine of musket balls passing nearby through the ever-increasing cloud of smoke enveloping the defense line. Each time a cannon fired, those close enough might twitch as the concussion of air whacked their eardrums. After a number of minutes of constant firing, muskets accumulate residue from the exploding black powder, fouling key parts of the armament. As the men had to spend extra moments cleaning the priming pan and touch-hole, their rate of fire would slow. Worry that one's musket would clog and thus become unusable greatly added to the overall tension of battle. As a corporal, Timothy would try to ignore the inevitable thudding of musket balls into the wooden barricade to his front and concentrate instead on the continual firing of the men around him.

Early in the battle, General Johnson was hit in the leg by a musket ball and carried back to a hospital tent. General Lyman took over command and bravely moved along the line, inspiring the men with his steadfast commands. He determined what part of the line was most threatened and quickly moved there to urge on the men in their defense. Lyman seemed protected by God, for even though his horse was killed, he remained untouched by enemy fire. His voice was reduced to a hoarse whisper, but his presence held the line. By about four o'clock in the afternoon, even the courageous French grenadiers had given up hope of victory, and the determined Dieskau lay wounded. Many in the English line sensed that the tide had turned and, without orders, leapt over their breastworks and pursued the enemy into the woods, smashing those they caught with hatchets and musket butts. The French retreat turned into a rout, as they left behind much of their equipment, dead, and wounded, including General Dieskau.

It was a great triumph for the English; drained smiles surely formed on the smudged faces of the sweaty and overall exhausted soldiers around Timothy.

The days after the battle were melancholy as the dead were buried, and the survivors cleaned the area of all the debris and waste of war. The sickening smell of death permeated the air. The three Connecticut companies in the pay of New York, which included Timothy's company, listed seven killed, one wounded, and three missing as casualties from the Battle of Lake George. This was fewer than were reported by some of the other units from New England; the men in Timothy's company had been lucky. Johnson's army, including the Mohawk allies, had total casualties listed as one hundred fifty-two killed, ninety-two wounded, and sixty-two missing.[25] The areas around the hospital tents in camp were filled with gruesome sights. Men with bloodied bandages wrapped around their wounds lay about, along with buckets full of amputated limbs. Many more casualties had been found in the forest. A small pond near the morning ambush had taken on a red hue from the accumulated blood therein of the dead and wounded. Ever since, it has been called Bloody Pond. Near the pond, some of the English bodies showed evidence of having been bound as prisoners, but later killed as the enemy fled. As this news of murdered prisoners spread through the army, the somber mood turned more furious.

After cleaning up the battlefield, the army returned to the construction of the fort. General Lyman had argued for an advance against the French, to take advantage of their victory. But Johnson refused. It took a whole week before Johnson even ordered men to scout the French at Ticonderoga. By that time, many of the Mohawk warriors had left for home carrying their spoils of war, so the provincials had to take over more of the scouting duties, along with the construction projects and guard duty. One group that emerged to perform the scouting duties superbly was the Rangers. They were led by Captain

Robert Rogers, from New Hampshire, and were manned predominately by those who lived on the frontiers of the colonies. Used to surviving in the wilderness through their hunting and tracking skills, they were natural scouts.

On the 16th of September a report came in that the French were again advancing against the camp at Lake George. It proved to be false, but disrupted the construction duties of the men. Ensuing, on the twentieth at midnight, an alarm mustered the whole army into formation to face an expected attack. This once again was false and further fatigued the hardworking soldiers. As the season advanced, the need for food, blankets, and proper winter clothing was becoming acute. The fish available in the lake were not enough to feed the whole army. The winter came early to Lake George, and the men were dressed only in their worn-out summer clothing. The first frost came on the night of September 25, after it had rained earlier that day. The men only had canvas tents over their heads and muddy ground under them. Timothy and his damp company mates suffered greatly when the frost hit. Sleep was very difficult under such conditions, and the lack of it made the days of labor that much harder.

The construction of Fort William Henry along the shore of Lake George involved massive digging, and plenty of wood. The fort was designed to repel an assault by infantry and to protect cannon from enemy artillery fire. With the use of hand tools, a wide ditch was dug outside the walls of the fort; the excavated soil was then used to fill the walls. The earth was held in place by tree trunks laid upon one another to form the inside and outside enclosures. These walls became over ten feet high and varied in thickness from about thirty feet at the foundation to about sixteen feet at the parapet, where the defending cannon were placed. It was designed to house a garrison of a few hundred men and thus was of considerable size.

The colonial governments had sent hundreds of reinforcements to the army at Lake George in the hope of continuing an advance to Crown Point, but this did not happen. In fact, some of the reinforcements were sent home. The frustration of the soldiers there began to boil. The men toiled long hours during the day and then shared guard duty during the night. They suffered through foul weather without proper equipment and cooked meager rations of food, when it was available. They had beaten the French in battle, but still they had not reached their goal of attacking Crown Point. Word came in the form of letters from home, or scarce newspapers, that the lack of progress of their army was questioned by the public at large as well.[26] The morale of Timothy's company most likely declined sharply.

On October 8, a tremendous storm hit the camp. Slashing raindrops and hail pelted the men, lightning struck a tree in camp, and the cruel wind blew another tree down, injuring a few men. Most of the next twenty-three days of October were cold, rainy, or snowy[27]—miserable conditions for life in camp with simple canvas tents. By the beginning of November, some of the soldiers had been released to go home. The resentment felt by those stuck in camp increased; certainly Timothy found it harder to control the men, especially when he could most likely sympathize with their feelings. It had been many long months since Timothy had seen Mary, not to mention the rest of his family. During the night of November 9, rain and hail soured their mood yet further. The next day a large number of Connecticut troops mutinied and prepared to leave, but they were ultimately convinced to stay by their pleading officers.

The next morning a cold mist hung over the camp as another mutiny of New Yorker troops occurred. But the camp's mood changed abruptly when Indian scouts reported that a large enemy force was approaching. Artillery pieces were dragged into the nearly completed fort, and breastworks around the camp were strengthened. The report was a false alarm, and the morale of the army dropped yet again. At four o'clock on the morning of November 14, the whole army again woke to still another false alarm. The next day, Captain Israel Putnam, a ranger from Connecticut, sent word from a scouting mission that he had found no French army anywhere, only making the flurry of recent alarms all the more frustrating.

The monotonous life of construction duty, guard duty, and patrolling was finally broken on November 18, at three in the morning, as the soldiers' world shook. The severe earthquake experienced by the men was felt by people in most of eastern North America. The sound of the quake might well have reminded Timothy of the mysterious cracks and rumbles that emanated on occasion from under the hills near his family's home in East Haddam. This extraordinary event was overshadowed that evening when a rare shipment of bread arrived in camp for the hungry soldiers.[28]

Still, the unease in the ranks of the army was overwhelming. Mutiny, or talk of it, was surely pervasive. Finally, on November 25, the commanders met to decide what part of the army would garrison Fort William Henry all winter, and who would be released to go home. The inch of snow covering the camp that morning added weight to the decision. Rumors flowed and anxiety reigned as the men struggled to warm themselves. It was finally decided that a small number of soldiers from each colony would be chosen to share the thankless service. Timothy must have been greatly relieved to find out he was not one of those chosen. He packed his belongings and broke camp a few cold days later. The march south to Albany fortunately moved much faster than had the grueling trek north that summer. Timothy was officially discharged from military service on December 2 to enjoy his reunion with Mary and his family.[29]

That winter, Timothy undoubtedly relished home-cooked meals and his warm bed. As difficult as life was on a New England farm, it must have seemed much easier to Timothy upon his return. He met his new baby sister, Elizabeth, born on July 19, 1755, but shared in his older brother's loss when his baby boy died on January 12, 1756.[30] The boy had not survived to see his first birthday, which would have been only four days later.

Timothy shared his experiences with family and friends, describing the strange dress and customs of the Indians he had witnessed, and relishing in the victory of the colonials at the Battle of Lake George. September 8 would become a sacred date for the veterans of the battle; ceremonies were held on that date even twenty years later, during the next war in America. Memories of the event would be passed down from generation to generation in doggerel ballads or crude lines of verse that were sung or recited around the fireside. One such ballad recorded the Battle of Lake George in the following way:

> The Summer now is past away,
> And then Comes on a bloody Day;
> They go to meet and so do Spy
> The faces of the Enemy.
>
> A furious fight Comes on a main
> And many Valiant men are slain;
> Of all the Battles now the third
> Was fought with garments rol'd in Blood.
>
> A frightful Noise & hideous yell,
> As tho it Came from the Jaws of Hell;
> The smoke did as a Cloud arise,
> While Christian prayers did pierce the Skies.
>
> And God did hear when they did Call
> And Anti-Christ receiv'd a fall.
> O may she bleed & Also die,
> That Christ may gain the Victory.
>
> They Quit the field with shameful flight,
> As tho they saw it dark as Night.
> Our men did plunder on the place,
> And Smiles returned in their face.[31]

CHAPTER 2

Waste of War

Over the winter of 1755–1756, Timothy and Mary received word of an increase of Indian raids along the frontiers of the English colonies. Reports of English colonists being tortured, killed, and stolen into captivity increased dramatically.[32] This had happened during the last war with France but, at that time, Timothy had been just a boy. Now he had a wife to worry about and many more responsibilities. Timothy, of course, was well acquainted with the blood-chilling war whoops of the Indians during battle and would certainly want to shield his family from those terrors.

Mary's family had experienced the horrors of Indian warfare, too. Eighty years earlier, her great-grandfather, Samuel Fuller, had been killed fighting the Indians during a war that ravaged New England. Lieutenant Fuller was ambushed, along with eighty others in Captain Michael Pierce's company, on March 26, 1676, near Rehoboth, Massachusetts. Nearly a thousand

Indians surrounded them and attacked. The men formed a circle and bravely fought for two hours until almost all were killed by the Indians. Nine more were taken alive and gruesomely tortured to death. Only eight survivors made it back to town to deliver the horrible news.[33] Mary's grandfather was born six months later and grew up without his father.[34]

During the spring of 1756, the Connecticut Assembly again requested volunteers for military service. In the last year, two Connecticut regiments had been raised, but in 1756 the plan was more ambitious—four regiments would be formed. Timothy could not help but notice that the goal of the campaign remained the same as the year before—the still-unattained capture of Crown Point. The Connecticut Assembly augmented the number of incentives to volunteer that year. Wages were inflated so that a corporal would be paid thirty-three shillings and six pence per month, a five-shilling increase from the year before. Further, a bounty of thirty-six shillings was to be paid to each soldier when he enlisted, and his first month's wages were to be advanced immediately. A special effort was made to reenlist experienced veterans from the year before. The Assembly also authorized those veterans who did sign up again to be paid half wages due their military rank from December 17, 1755, until the day of their reenlistment.[35]

Most of Timothy's memories from the previous campaign would have recalled tedious duties, strenuous labor, inconsistent food supplies, hostile bugs and challenging weather, and the overall horror of war. After experiencing those conditions, he probably relished more than ever the tranquil time he spent at home, making any decision to leave again that much harder. Yet something had to be done to stop the French and Indian war parties ravaging the frontiers, and the money he would earn could balance the risks. This time the money that would be paid to him upon enlistment could be left with Mary and provide greater aid for her while he was away. His decision was made accordingly, and, after completing as much of the spring planting as possible, he and Gershom Rowley volunteered again on May 13. This time he was made a sergeant in Captain Edmund Wells's company in the Fourth Connecticut Regiment.[36] After he collected his half pay since December plus his bounty and the first month's pay, the total was seven pounds, seventeen shillings—a very generous sum in those days for a man like Timothy.[37] Needless to say, despite such an inflated sum, the goodbyes were likely difficult for the whole family and trepidations about the days ahead at least equally arduous.

Captain Wells's company set sail for Albany from the Connecticut River in the middle of June. The men passed through Long Island Sound, past Manhattan Island, and proceeded up the Hudson River. They arrived at Albany on July 1 and joined the other provincial troops marshalling for the renewed Crown Point campaign. Captain Edmund Wells was a thirty-five-year-old carpenter and farmer from Hebron, Connecticut.[38] An older sergeant in the company named Orlando Mack, from Hebron as well, worked alongside Timothy to prepare their men for the coming ordeal. (Years later, in 1768, Orlando's son would marry Anna Fuller, from East Haddam, who was a distant relative of Timothy's wife.[39]) Throughout early July, they organized military units, collected provisions, and drilled the soldiers. Guarding the camps day and night became their routine, once again. Some evenings they might sing hymns or listen to Orlando Mack argue religious points about men's souls.[40] They encountered the usual delays, but this time the delays emanated from a dearth in overall command as well. In the spring, England and France had declared war against each other, officially starting the Seven Years' War. A new English commander, John Campbell, Earl of Loudoun, was put in command of all military operations in North America. But he did not arrive in New York until July 22. With the encroaching fall weather, a significant part of the campaign season had expired well before he even took charge.

Timothy's company started marching toward Fort Edward on July 15, guarding artillery and provision wagons along the way. The hot, humid weather and relentless insects must have tortured the men. On the evening of July 18, allied

Indians conducted a war dance near their camp. Through this ceremonial dance, warriors interpreted past deeds of valor, incorporating the physical actions of combat. The painted bodies of the warriors adorned with feathers and jewelry would gyrate with motions imitating striking their foes or throwing their tomahawks.[41] The men in Timothy's company must have been fascinated by this display of foreign culture and may also have suppressed their latent fears as the sound of Indian whoops and screams spread through the dark forest around them. In addition to these foreign performances, Timothy and his men were startled by another new encounter in the brutal form of eighteenth-century military justice. On the nineteenth, two men were each given one hundred lashes on their backs as punishment for mutiny. But life moved on and by the twenty-second, they had set up a more permanent camp at Fort Edward.[42] The earthen and log fort was situated where the Hudson River makes a sharp right turn, heading south toward Albany. The main part of the fort was on the eastern bank, but many of the soldiers camped on the largest island in the middle of the river. This was the base for the group known as the Rangers—the hard-drinking and troublesome scouts who were under the command of Major Rogers. This tough bunch would travel over forest, lake, and stream, scouting the wilderness for weeks at a time, fighting French and Indians along the way. Their individualistic frontier lifestyle made them very self-sufficient woodsmen, but also made them extremely difficult to contain in a camp. The Rangers adopted some of the dress of Indians most suited for trekking through the forest; many also left their faces unshaven and generally lacked the manners of most men from Connecticut. In many ways, therefore, the Rangers must have been as strange to Timothy and the others as the Indians they had witnessed.[43]

At Fort Edward, Timothy's company faced the tedious duties of both guarding the fort and escorting supply wagons traveling to Fort William Henry on the shore of Lake George. On July 29 they labored to improve the fortifications around Fort Edward. Then they spent the thirty-first chasing lost cattle in the woods. In so doing, they roamed the woods in the rain and got lost for a while, but in the end collected at least fifteen of the cattle. Fortunately they did not meet any hostile Indians while they were divided into smaller groups for the hunt. There had been reports of the enemy in the area, and during the week prior, two teamsters had been scalped, precisely while herding cattle. Captain Wells reassembled his search party and led the soaked group back to Fort Edward. As the sky cleared in the afternoon, they must have hoped to dry their clothes. But their desires were spoiled by a severe thunderstorm that poured all night.[44]

An important new aspect of the 1756 campaign was the introduction of regular British soldiers.[45] The Forty-eighth Regiment marched through the area in July.[46] The soldiers of the regiment wore white clothing under their red coats. Their black tricorn hats were decorated with white trim and their regimental coats accented with buff.[47] The homogeneous uniforms of the Forty-eighth contrasted greatly with the Connecticut troops' mix of varied provincial regimental coats and civilian clothes. In addition, the British soldiers marched in step together and performed their drills crisply. Their discipline was beyond anything the provincial troops had ever witnessed. As the campaign progressed, more regular regiments joined the provincials. The strict, regular army officers expected their soldiers to obey their every whim (like servants) and distributed painful physical punishments to ensure the soldiers' future obedience. The officers brought with them enormous bags filled with luxuries that Timothy, as well as many of the provincial officers, would never have foreseen. Overall, the differences between the British officers and soldiers were striking to the provincials.

The different command styles of the provincials and the regulars led to more delays. The provincial General John Winslow, from Massachusetts, commander of all the New England troops on the Crown Point expedition, expressed the concerns of his men to General Loudoun shortly after he arrived in North America. There were two British military policies that particularly upset the provincials. The first ranked all provincial officers junior to regular officers. This meant that General Winslow could actually be commanded by a young captain in the regulars. The second placed all provincial forces acting in conjunction with regular units to be under the same military law and discipline as the regulars. Winslow warned that, considering the temperament of his men, these policies might cause the provincials to quit and go home. Loudoun offered a concession on the first policy, allowing provincial generals and colonels to act as senior captains in the regular army. Still, many of the New England officers, who had more experience fighting in North American campaigns than the regulars, felt this conciliatory gesture was hollow. The situation grew very tense. The provincials were dedicated to the defeat of France, but their resistance to official military regulations was considered sedition. The impasse was settled by the middle of August when Loudoun asked the provincial officers to sign a written promise to serve the regular military in exchange for a verbal promise of the segregation of regular troops from colonials whenever possible during the campaign. This did not solve the problem, but it did force the New Englanders to declare, in written form, their intent to serve the British command.[48]

Meanwhile, Timothy and the men in his company continued their duties at Fort Edward. After ten o'clock on the night of August 2, his company was called into formation. The men were joined by men from other companies as they checked their weapons and equipment. The force of three hundred soldiers marched out of camp at eleven in pursuit of enemy Indians who were reportedly near Fort William Henry. They marched quietly for about three or four miles in the dark until they met an enemy ambush. In an instant, the woods were afire with musket blasts. The Indians yelled, and the provincials howled in return. It was too confusing to notice who was hurt or even where everyone had taken cover. The musket fire continued for only five minutes. As quickly as it had started, the skirmish ended. They stayed there all night curled up among the roots and branches on the forest floor.

Those on guard struggled to see or hear any sign of a renewed attack. Those trying to sleep kept their muskets close by, loaded and primed. Everyone most likely fought off the mosquitoes, an ever-present annoyance in the woods of New York. At first light, Captain Wells inspected the area around their position and found evidence that the enemy had been on both sides of the trail during the night's ambush. To his surprise, only one man in their party had been killed, and four wounded. The men arose with aching bodies and tired eyes. After arrangements were made to take the casualties back to Fort Edward, they continued their search. The tracks of the Indians were followed for a few miles, but none of the elusive enemy was found, so they were ordered back to Fort Edward. But shortly thereafter, they did stumble upon the enemy again. Two shots were fired and men on both sides recommenced the yelling and whooping. The provincials charged as one group, running up a hill in pursuit. The enemy dared not stand, and fled, abandoning two wagons of provisions. No enemy dead were found, but blood trails led away from the site; therefore, it was assumed at least some were wounded. Fortunately, the rest of the trip back to the fort was quiet, and Wells thanked God for their safe return.[49]

Timothy's company marched out for another scout on the afternoon of August 16. The weather was pleasant and clear. The group numbered about 450, comprising a collection of companies under the command of Colonel Fitch, of the First Connecticut Regiment. The first two nights were quiet, except for some drunken soldiers creating a commotion in camp. On the eighteenth, they started early and reached the South Bay area of Lake Champlain by about one o'clock. The men took a break along the lake, which is nestled among rock cliffs and mountains. Later in the afternoon, about half the party headed back to Fort Edward, while Timothy's company continued on to Wood Creek. The men kept a fast pace until they approached an exceedingly steep hill. Their hard leather shoes caused many to slip while ascending. The leather straps across Timothy's shoulders and chest would have dug into his body as his clothes became increasingly drenched in sweat. He surely grabbed branches and rocks to help his difficult progress up the slope. Each breath strained the capacity of the lungs. Upon surmounting the hill, they found that their route continued up still more hills until they finally stopped to camp after sunset. Fortunately no alarm disturbed their sleep that night.[50]

The next morning, the nineteenth, they stretched their stiff limbs and started fires for a simple meal. They started about ten in the morning, and ascended more hills and slopes for over two hours. They stopped often to catch their breath. The top of one hill was finally reached through a narrow passage in the rock; a long break was ordered for the men. Their descent that afternoon followed small ponds and streams where Timothy could refresh himself with the cool water. While most of the afternoon's route was downhill they still had to climb a bit, and the last part of the day became very difficult due to numerous fallen trees blocking their progress. Another quiet night helped them recover.[51]

After three and a half days of marching, the men were feeling worn out. In the morning it was noticeable that Colonel Fitch was looking poorly as well. Captain Wells was in better spirits though, and carved his name, the month, and the year on a nearby tree.[52] Everyone's muscles ached as they put on their packs and equipment to start another day that would be a repeat of the one before. Fortunately, no one in the company had trouble with the numerous rattlesnakes that could be found in these forests.[53] On the twenty-first they arose much as they had the previous mornings, with tea warming on the fire, but at least they were closer to their return to Fort Edward. The weather was fine and they started out early, around seven. Shortly after they began, Henry Smith, a man in Timothy's company, collapsed and was too ill to keep up with the march. Being close to the fort, the company split up. Captain Wells and a small group helped Smith continue the journey, while a majority continued with Colonel Fitch. When the main column reached the camp at Fort Edward they sent a horse back to carry Smith the rest of the way. The next day Timothy and his men recovered from their exertions. The weather was fine, and they tried to clean their filthy clothes and muskets. In the evening, a party of Mohawks returned to the camp proudly displaying two French scalps they had taken.[54] For the uninitiated in Timothy's company, the trophies of hair and skin with dried blood were a gruesome example of Indian warfare.

August 23 was another clear, beautiful day, but the weather was forgotten with the news of the French capture of Fort Oswego.[55] The men in camp were besieged by more rumors and consequent worries, and with questions that neither Timothy nor any other officer could answer. The generals were concerned by the news. Fort Oswego was the westernmost in a chain of forts built to guard the east–west route between Lake Ontario and Albany. The capture of this fort by the new French commander in North America, General Louis-Joseph Montcalm, seemed to indicate an invasion of New York from the west. In response, the English commanders changed their plans from the offensive to the defensive.

Timothy's company returned to the daily routine of guard duty and laboring on fortifications. As August advanced into September, the lack of progress toward capturing Crown Point frustrated the provincials and the health of the army deteriorated. Many in Timothy's company fell sick and were declared unfit for duty. Those strong enough to work constructed a hospital in camp. Some of the sick in the company were sent back to Albany for better care. The graveyard at Fort Edward grew in size almost every day as disease claimed the lives of more and more soldiers. The number of desertions increased as well. On the evening of September 20, the entire Fourth Connecticut Regiment was mustered into formation. Of the over six hundred men who had started this campaign, only eighty-nine were healthy enough to answer the roll call. Captain Wells was ill, and his mood had become sullen. He made frequent visits to the graveyard and counted a total of 137 graves by September 27. The next day the company marched away from Fort Edward toward Fort William Henry. Timothy's company started the campaign with seventy-seven men, but only twenty-eight marched to Fort William Henry.[56] Timothy's health may have deteriorated as well, for he and eleven others from the company were discharged early on October 16.[57]

As Timothy recovered at home, bad news of the war could be read in the newspapers. The confrontation had widened to embrace many parts of the world, and England's new ally, Prussia, had suffered a number of defeats as well. The empires of France, Austria, and Russia were aligned against England and Prussia. Taxes in Connecticut increased to pay for the war, and trade suffered when General Loudoun issued an embargo in March 1757. All colonial ships were restricted unless on official military business. There had been reports of merchants trading with the French, and Loudoun meant to end that practice. Yet the edict punished all merchants, and the communities that benefited from the sea trade. The embargo did not last all year, but the colonists did not forget the damage it caused.

Loudoun also changed the organization of the provincial forces. Each colony would raise only one regiment in 1757, thus limiting the number of officers above the rank of captain, and eliminating any provincial ranks of general. The terms of service for the provincials required they work directly with, and under the command and discipline of, the regular army. Loudoun's actions greatly soured relations between the colonials and the British military. Connecticut called for volunteers for the 1757 campaign, and many known to Timothy signed on again. Captain Wells, Sergeant Mack, and thirteen men from East Haddam joined the eleventh company in the one Connecticut regiment. The colonel was Phineas Lyman, who had been a general the year before. Timothy declined to join the campaign, likely balancing the risks to his health, the time away from Mary, and the needs of maintaining a family farm against the wages he could earn. He was not alone in this decision. Many declined, and at least one family (from Colchester) sent its slave rather than a family member to serve in Captain Wells's company.[58]

Wells's company marched off to war at the end of April. This year the soldiers walked all the way to Fort Edward, where they were stationed for the whole campaign. Timothy could search the war reports in the newspapers for anything that would indicate how they were faring. The provincials garrisoned the forts with a small number of regular troops, while Loudoun led most of the regulars on an expedition against the fortress town of Louisbourg. Delays in assembling the invasion force, bad weather, and timely French reinforcements to Louisbourg all combined to cancel the proposed attack, but the British troops earmarked for this endeavor were away from the New York frontier for most of the campaign season.

The French had assembled an army eight thousand strong at Fort Carillon, on the Ticonderoga peninsula. Included in this force were 1,600 Indians from all over French Canada and as far away as the western plains of North America. General Montcalm meant to use this army to attack the English at the Great Carrying Place. Montcalm started the advance south along Lake George on July 30 with a part of his army marching along the western shore. The rest of the army moved south on the lake the next day. The Indians, adorned in shades of red, black, and blue dyes, and crested in feathery headdresses, led the way in over one hundred birch-bark canoes. Over two hundred small boats followed, carrying the French regulars. Each regiment was identified by red or blue facings on its white uniforms. Some boats were linked together, creating broad wooden decks to carry the heavy artillery pieces necessary to blast the walls of the English forts.

Montcalm's army reached Fort William Henry on August 3 and quickly took up positions all around the English. Lieutenant Colonel George Monro commanded 2,800 English soldiers at Lake George, of whom only eight hundred were regulars. The area commander at Fort Edward, General Daniel Webb, had another two thousand, most of whom were provincials. So as the French started a formal siege of Fort William Henry they had the advantages of greater numbers and the better position, having split the opposing forces in two. The only hope Monro had of holding his position was for Webb to advance with a relief force that could assist in driving back the French. Webb needed more men to attempt a relief of Fort William Henry, and sent word to the colonies to raise more militia—and to send them quickly.

In East Haddam the alarm was sounded, and the local militia was notified of the great need to rescue the men at Fort William Henry. Timothy hurriedly assembled with seventy-five men from the town. Timothy served as a sergeant under the command of Captain Daniel Cone. They left town on August 9, and moved quickly; sixty-two of them rode horses to speed their march.[59] The roads in Connecticut were crowded with the thousands of men marching to the relief of the fort.[60] The Connecticut men started to arrive at Fort Edward on August 12, but their haste had been in vain; Fort William Henry had already surrendered.

By August 9 the situation at William Henry was dire. The fort's walls were battered; the supplies were nearly exhausted; most of the artillery pieces were unserviceable; and the garrison was exhausted from five nights of siege without rest. Monro's hopes of holding the fort longer were dashed when he learned of a captured dispatch intended for him. The message was from Webb, stating that Webb could not come to their aid and that Monro should surrender the fort. Since Montcalm possessed this information, surrender was the only option remaining for Monro. Considering the desperate situation facing the English, the terms for capitulation offered by Montcalm were gracious. The English would be allowed to keep their muskets, swords, and one cannon. If they agreed not to serve in the war for eighteen months they could march to Fort Edward, under French escort, and they would not become prisoners. The surrender was accepted, but the French lost control of their Indian allies. Indians started looting the fort as soon as the English marched out. Some of the sick and wounded, left behind under the care of the French, were killed. One Indian was observed carrying the severed head of one of these unfortunate souls. Later, as the English were marching to Fort Edward, the Indians swarmed around the column, and started grabbing backpacks, personal possessions, and finally people to take home as slaves. The situation deteriorated as many of the English scattered in panic and turned the affair into what was soon labeled a massacre. The survivors arrived at Fort Edward over the following days, while a few took even longer. The French demolished Fort William Henry and withdrew north.

The relief militia was sent home on August 17. Timothy made it home by August 24. That same day, Gershom Rowley's father died, and the next day his younger brother, Moses, died as well.[61] The neighborhood in the northwest corner of East Haddam was in a depressed state that autumn. The personal losses of family members combined with the constant woeful war news greatly lowered morale in East Haddam and across much of the British Empire by the end of 1757. Furthermore, Indians continued to raid English settlements all along the frontier. The other defeats in Europe and losses in America further worried families like the Percivals; they hoped the fortunes of the English empire would soon change.

CHAPTER 3
War's Pendulum

By the end of 1757 the English war effort had reached a definitive low point. The combination of military defeat and Loudoun's mishandling of both the provincial forces and colonial assemblies had deeply affected the colonists. Resistance to Loudoun grew. From the fall of 1757 through the winter of 1758, anti-recruitment riots occurred in Delaware, New Hampshire, Massachusetts, and Connecticut. Representatives of the New England colonies met in Boston in February to decide the number of troops to provide for the 1758 campaign, without even consulting with Loudoun. He responded by summoning all the New England governors to a meeting in Hartford, Connecticut, where he issued the dictate that he alone would decide how many soldiers would be supplied for the campaign.[62] The colonial assemblies avoided outright confrontation after that meeting, but their aversion was apparent in their subsequent limited cooperation.

The mishandling of the war effort, and the shameful defeats of the English military, invoked a change in England. Planning for the campaigns was taken over by William Pitt, a longtime member of Parliament who held the office of secretary of state. Many members of Parliament were politically connected with those held responsible for the mishandled war effort, and lost their political influence as a result. Many of the same had resisted Pitt in the past. This left Pitt unencumbered to put forward his plans for war and have them accepted by Parliament. The effect Pitt had on the British war effort was profound. He greatly increased the money sent to aid England's ally, Prussia, in fighting the European campaigns, while British regulars were used to fight the French elsewhere. The conquest of French Canada became a primary goal. Pitt also guaranteed the colonial governments that Parliament would reimburse them for their war expenditures. He then reversed the policy that limited all provincial officers to being mere captains in the regular army, instead decreeing that their ranks would be inferior only to the comparable regular-army rank. In other words, a provincial colonel would be outranked only by regular-army colonels, and so on. In addition, Loudoun was relieved of his command—to the colonists' great relief.

The change in the colonial attitude was dramatic. The New England assemblies immediately voted to increase their involvement in the war effort. The Connecticut Assembly authorized the raising of five thousand soldiers in March. The soldiers were organized into four regiments, and the Assembly nominated all the officers. Nathan Whiting, the hero of the Battle of Lake George, would be colonel of the Second Regiment. Joseph Spencer, of East Haddam, would raise a company of men for Whiting's regiment, and Timothy was appointed ensign in that company. It was an honor for Timothy to be entrusted with the position of an officer; he accepted the position on March 27.[63]

The first duty of the officers was to recruit and organize the men to serve that year. Timothy could earn a bonus of three shillings for each man he enlisted.[64] Since the farmers of East Haddam did not have much besides their land, the chance to earn money as a soldier was an incentive for many. The wages had been increased for this campaign, so that even a private could earn one pound, sixteen shillings each month. Timothy would earn three pounds, ten shillings per month as an ensign—twice his pay during his last campaign. To further induce men to enlist, Connecticut authorized four pounds sterling per man to properly equip them. Anyone who provided his own equipment that passed inspection by the officers would be paid the value of that equipment out of the four-pound allowance. Each man would also be provided with a blanket, a knapsack, and his first month's pay before leaving for the campaign.[65]

The chance to strike back at the despised Indian allies of the French, who continued to kill, burn, and steal along the frontier, was another alluring inducement to volunteer. The first man enlisted in Timothy's company on March 30. Later, on April 11, Timothy's comrade in arms, Gershom Rowley, joined the company.[66] In less than four weeks, the company consisted of eighty men. While the officers checked the men's equipment (or noted their lack of it), they continued to recruit. Although many men responded early in Connecticut, it was still difficult to fill the largest-to-date quota set by the Assembly. It took the officers over two months; they even enlisted men from neighboring towns to add to their eventual total of ninety-four. The company even included an Indian, William Tutson.[67]

Major Joseph Spencer's religious principles guided his command of those in his charge. He lived near his church in the Millington section of East Haddam and had a close relationship with Reverend Hobart Estabrook, the pastor of that church since November 1745.[68] So it was quite fitting for Estabrook to oblige the major's request to preach a special sermon to the entire company before it left for the campaign. The men assembled on Tuesday, May 30, to hear Estabrook's sermon, "The Praying Warrior." The pastor told them that it was "necessary," even "lawful," to go to war, that even good

Christians must fight. "When our lives, liberties and properties are directly threatened, and imminently exposed, we may take up arms in our defence [sic]," preached Estabrook. "[W]hen kingdoms and nations, do acts of violence, there is no other way to decide the controversy: The injured may take up the sword and fight, referring the decision of the controversy to the almighty." He then addressed Major Spencer, lieutenants Brainard and Harding, and Ensign Percival.

> We would hope ye are influenced to this important undertaking, from noble views, viz. the securing of the just rights, and liberties of your country, and the protection of these churches in the enjoyment of very precious privileges, all which are manifest[l]y threatened, by the insulting foes you expect to meet . . . [E]ndeavor to treat these your soldiers with tenderness, and at the same time keep up your proper authority and government. . . . Be bold for God, and let no impiety that properly falls under your cognizance, escape your censure, or pass unpunished. You will endeaver [sic] that they be subject to order, and attend the religious worship, for which there is good provision made. And now we wish you prosperity. Go forth in the name of the Lord: and in his name set up your banners: Trust in him, and refer all your concerns, with those of your dear families unto him.[69]

With these instructions weighing heavily on Timothy, he spent the last days at home preparing to leave. Once again Timothy had to say goodbye to Mary, hoping that this year the French would be defeated, finally ending the war. Timothy gathered with his company along the banks of the Connecticut River on June 6.[70] Before the men boarded ship, the roll was called, and it was noted that Abraham Warner, David Stocker, and Mathew Ransom were missing. The officers listed them as deserters and started the embarkation of the men.[71] Losing three men before the campaign started may have been perceived as a bad omen.

Fortunately the trip by water was uneventful, and they disembarked at Greenbush, New York, near Albany. Colonel Whiting was there waiting for his twelve companies from Connecticut, and he was glad to see Spencer's company arrive. The colonel ordered Major Spencer to lead his company to Fort Edward on June 15, while Whiting remained behind until the last of his companies appeared.[72] The plan was to assemble the largest North American army yet seen at Lake George, with the overarching goals of capturing Fort Carillon at Ticonderoga and Fort St. Frederic at Crown Point, then proceeding north to French Canada. General James Abercromby, the new English commander of operations in New York, worked diligently to procure the necessary supplies for such a large force, but found that it could not be done on schedule. It took time to transport seventeen thousand soldiers as well as to construct or purchase, and then move to Lake George, all the boxes of ammunition, casks of food, tents, cooking utensils, muskets, flints, and over one thousand boats. A convoy from England carrying ten thousand muskets, four thousand tents, and much-needed artillery did not arrive in New York until June 13, causing further delay. It also took a long time for the provincial troops to arrive from their respective colonies.[73]

The trip from Albany to Lake George was all too familiar for Timothy. It was a difficult sixty-three miles of water and road travel. North of Albany there were two difficult portages on the Hudson River. The first at Half Moon traversed a twelve-mile road. The second followed a road through the forest from Saratoga to Fort Edward, and then joined another road at the Great Carrying Place to Lake George. As the army moved north, the men helped move the supplies along the way. Every item had to be loaded and unloaded five times. Due to a shortage of draft animals, men sometimes took on the burden of dragging loads on the well-used and rutted roads.[74] The weather was awful. Nine of the last fourteen days of June were either hot and humid, or rainy and stormy, making Timothy and his men constantly wet from either perspiration or precipitation.[75] The heavy wooden boats, or bateaux as they were called, had to be transported over land as well. These were between twenty-five and thirty feet long, twelve feet wide, and capable of carrying twenty-two men.[76] Whether rowing or carrying the boats, the wet hands of the men blistered quickly. The cool nights caused the men to shiver in the early morning, but soon their toils soaked their clothes in sweat and that brief moment of feeling cold was but a fond memory.

The vast swarm of laboring humanity between Albany and Lake George was a colorful mixture. There were almost six thousand regulars, mostly in red regimental coats, but including the Eightieth Regiment with dark brown uniforms and black leather caps. The men of the Forty-second Royal Highland Regiment were there as well in short red coats, green kilts, red-and-white-checkered socks, and blue bonnets on their heads. The provincial regiments hailed from Massachusetts, Connecticut, New York, New Jersey, Rhode Island, and New Hampshire. Then there was the Corps of Bateauxmen, 1,600 provincials led by Lieutenant Colonel John Bradstreet, who had recruited and trained them to both fight as soldiers and handle boats to transport supplies on the wilderness waterways. Under Robert Rogers, four hundred of the ill-disciplined but valuable Rangers were there to scout in search of the enemy. Stockbridge Indians from western Massachusetts were also part of the corps, as were four hundred Mohawk warriors, led by Sir William Johnson, commander of the English army at the Battle of Lake George. Importantly, this would be the first campaign in the war where Indians allied to the English outnumbered those allied to the French.[77] Many of the Indians who fought with the French at Fort William Henry in 1757 actually brought home more than scalps and prisoners—smallpox followed them home to their villages, making death rampant and ultimately persuading most of the survivors to stay home in 1758.[78]

The second in command of the English army, General George Howe, brought a new sense of vitality and service that united the varied backgrounds of the English army. In the past, most British officers had bogged down the campaigns with the trappings of their higher social status. Extra clothes, fine drink, and other items to entertain others of the upper class added to the size of their baggage that had to be hauled through the wilderness. Howe was different. Soon after his arrival in North America, he abandoned the traditional army training and drill, observing that it had no place on the American frontier. Instead, he studied wilderness fighting with the Indians and the Rangers. Howe then used this knowledge to train his regiment, the Fifty-fifth, in the art of fighting and surviving in the forests. He also changed the uniforms of his regiment to suit their new tasks as light infantry. The stylish tricorn hats, lace, bright colors, and long coats were thrown away or adjusted. Long hair was cut, shiny muskets were dulled, and leggings were worn to protect from the underbrush. Hardly an elitist, Howe washed his own clothes himself, slept with one blanket and bearskin, and ate the same food as the soldiers. He carried only what was essential to perform his military duties, refraining from the luxuries other officers tried to retain. For this campaign, he issued orders that transformed the officers, and soldiers, to a closer likeness of his example.[79] Even the skeptical provincials grew to trust and follow Howe without question. Most likely, Timothy and the others could sense a new emboldened spirit among the troops. It took some time, but they were gathering a massive, united force on the southern shore of Lake George. They hoped to finally advance to Crown Point, defeating the enemy along the way.

The companies of the Second Connecticut Regiment assembled and set up camp at Lake George by June 28.[80] They were the first provincial regiment to arrive there and joined the regular troops in preparations for the next stage of the advance. The men rolled enough lead ball and black powder in paper to make thirty-six cartridges for each soldier.[81] Food was prepared, and provisions, casks of powder, and extra flints loaded on the boats. Those boats damaged on the rough journey from Albany had to be caulked and repaired. Heavy mortars and cannon were manhandled onto large wooden rafts, nicknamed "floating castles."[82] Timothy saw the camp grow as more regiments arrived. The shore of the lake was swallowed up by a sea of white tents and loaded boats. The broken and charred remains of Fort William Henry contrasted sharply against the linear rows of tents housing thousands of eager new fighters. The ruins were undoubtedly a constant reminder to Timothy and the others of the excruciating French victory the year before, not to mention of the long-laboring days of erecting that fort three years prior. After a lengthy, hot and humid July 3 filled with the duties of their many preparations, Timothy heard a bagpiper from the Highlander regiment play a strange tune that echoed among the mountains on both sides of the lake.[83] They were almost ready to advance, and the future was uncertain for them all.

The advance up Lake George started on July 4, even though the whole army had still not assembled. The hot temperature and very cloudy skies threatened to produce a storm; fortunately, no disruption from the weather occurred. The lead units loaded onto their boats and rowed about a mile before halting for the night. This movement was necessary to make more room for the units scheduled to embark the next morning. At daybreak on the fifth, the drums echoed across the lake signaling what was to be the beginning of a very long day.

The army was divided into three divisions, the regulars were in the center, and the provincials formed the flanks on either side. The army was led by the Rangers, the Bateauxmen, and the light infantry of the regulars. Each regiment had an appointed time to approach the beach and load into its assigned boats. The whole process had been thought out ahead of time, and every detail planned. Timothy's regiment had a position further back in the army so he had time to observe much of the operation. The columns of soldiers with their muskets held up on their shoulders could be described as looking like many fuzzy caterpillars inching their way toward the lake. Upon reaching the water's edge each section would embark on a boat, and, as the oars moved in unison, pull away from the shore. Timothy's company soon lost sight of the lake as the huge flotilla completely covered the clear sparkling water. The bright sun highlighted the colors of the uniforms, the flash of moving oars, and the varied green hues of the birch and pine trees covering the islands and mountains on each side. Resounding notes of different military instruments bounced back and forth off the towering sides of the valley until not one tune could be distinguished in the jumble of sound. Altogether, it was an unforgettable sight for all those involved.[84]

It was surely as remarkable to the French scouts observing from their positions high in the woods. Abercromby's army was almost three times larger than the army France had sent south the year before. At Fort Carillon, General Montcalm was made painfully aware of this fact from his scouts' reports. Montcalm's situation looked bleak. Not only was he outnumbered four-to-one, he was also short of food and other supplies.[85] His scouts dutifully sent reports, informing him that the English had stopped for the night near the northern end of the lake, still south of the French positions. It appeared that the leading elements of the English army had unloaded, set up tents, and started fires, but this was actually a ruse created by General Howe, who commanded the advance guard. By eleven at night, the English were back in the water, and rowing north.[86]

The early dawn light was still quite dim when the Rangers and light infantry of the regulars approached the French positions at the northern end of the thirty-two-mile-long lake. The French there were completely surprised and scrambled to collect as much of their camp equipment as they could before fleeing north. The landing area was secured and the English army spent the morning disembarking.[87] At about noon Howe led his light infantry forward with the Rangers and the regulars. The provincial units followed as they disembarked. The area through which Howe advanced was a thick, dark stretch of forest where the ground changed levels abruptly. Visibility was reduced to yards in the thick underbrush and maze of fallen timber. The units stumbling through this section quickly became lost and confused.[88]

Through this tangle of woods west of the river connecting Lake George and Lake Champlain, a French scouting party of 350 quickly moved toward Fort Carillon. They had been cut off by the English surprise move during the night, and were trying to escape around the encroaching army. Both sides met in a fierce skirmish. Timothy's Second Connecticut Regiment was too far back in the advancing army to take part, but there were men from the First and Third Connecticut regiments as well as Rangers from Connecticut involved. English units moved as quickly as the terrain allowed toward the sound of musket fire, and the French had to retire, fighting from tree to tree, to avoid being surrounded. The French withdrew to the river, where many jumped into the surging water, swollen by the heavy rains in late June. It was a desperate attempt to escape, for large numbers were either shot while struggling in the water or drowned. Nearly 150 of the French were rounded up in the woods and made prisoners.[89]

It was a victory for the English, but they had no idea of the scope of the French defeat. The smoke discharged from the muskets seeped through the tangled forest, reducing visibility still further as dusk settled on the scene. In the ranks of many provincial units, it seemed possible that the entire French army was attacking. The English advance slowed to a halt as officers tried to figure out where they were and what to do next. Howe had been killed instantly by a musket ball in the first few minutes of action, and his leadership would be sorely missed. As news of his death spread through the army, the whole operation seemed to grind to a slow crawl. The Second Connecticut disembarked that day amid the artillery and supplies unloaded on the shore, but the army did not advance. The men huddled together in the woods with their muskets close, guarding against a sudden attack and trying to rest.[90]

July 7 dawned with cloudy weather, but the French hardly noticed as they worked feverishly on their defenses. They placed tree trunks on one another to form a wall high enough to protect standing soldiers, and laid the broken branches on the ground in front of the wall. The sharpened branches formed a very effective obstacle.[91] They knew their only chance of success relied on the quick construction of this defense line. Each French regiment prominently displayed its flag on its section of the line, and set to work in true earnest. Even some of the officers labored, spurring on their men.[92]

Meanwhile, the morning of July 7 was less decisive for Abercromby. He held a council with his officers, and finally decided on a proposal, put forward by Bradstreet, to advance along the road toward the fort. Bradstreet assembled a mixed force of regulars from the Forty-fourth and Sixtieth regiments, two Massachusetts regiments, Rangers, and two cannon. By early afternoon he had led them to a partially destroyed bridge over the La Chute River, where a sawmill stood. They immediately started repairs on the bridge, but the day ended before they advanced further.[93] That evening Timothy's regiment struggled in the dark to haul two cannon and the artillery equipment up to the position at the sawmill. They passed other units carrying torches heading back to the landing.[94] A small rain shower during the day meant the soggy soft ground made their endeavors that much harder.

That evening Abercromby had to decide whether to storm the French position with infantry, or bring up his heavy artillery and mortars, and prepare for a long siege. He decided on a massive infantry assault the next morning based on reports that the French defensive positions looked unfinished, and that the French were to be reinforced soon with three thousand men. Unfortunately, none of these reports were accurate. The French had camouflaged their positions so that the completed parts of the works were not visible, and the reinforcements were merely four hundred men who arrived the evening of July 7. These reinforcements were greeted enthusiastically by the tired Frenchmen and boosted their morale, but in reality they did not change the odds much at all.[95]

Timothy awoke the morning of July 8 to pleasant, breezy weather. He and his men were most likely still tired, their bodies aching, but that was displaced by the excitement and trepidation of imminent battle. They had more time than other units to prepare their morning meal because their regiment would be part of the rear guard assembling later. The order of advance was divided into four lines. The first included the Rangers, Bateauxmen, and Eightieth Regiment of light infantry. As these men advanced, they spread out in skirmish formation to find the enemy and prevent an ambush. They were followed by the enormous New York regiment made up of three battalions, each about the size of the other regiments, and the six Massachusetts regiments. In the third line were the six regular regiments who would bear the responsibility of the main assault. General Lyman's division formed the last line with the Rhode Island and New Jersey regiments on the left, and the four Connecticut regiments in the center and right.[96] The morning was spent forming these four lines and cautiously advancing toward the French. Around nine o'clock, Johnson's Mohawk Indians started whooping and firing on the French positions from Rattlesnake Mountain across the river to the south. They were too far away, though, and did not have any effect on the battle.[97]

Around noon the skirmishers of both armies found each other, and the battle began. The Rangers in front of the New York troops chased away the French pickets to their front. As the Rangers followed the enemy to the right, they left the New York regiment vulnerable, advancing without skirmishers in front to warn them. The New York men advanced into more enemy skirmishers, and with a loud cheer they drove the French away. The commander of the left brigade of regulars mistook this cheer for an advance on the main French line, and ordered his Twenty-seventh and Sixtieth regiments to quickly attack in support of the New Yorkers. Their advance stumbled directly into the sharpened branches strewn over the ground in front of the French line. They struggled through the tangle of tree limbs. Their leather straps and other equipment got caught in the branches, and all order collapsed.[98]

Abercromby had planned to have his regulars attack together along the whole line, but now they advanced, fell back and regrouped, then attacked again based on decisions made by the three regular brigade commanders on the field. The felled trees along the entire front of the French line destroyed all cohesion in the English advance. As the men jumped over and threaded through the branches, they fell over their own dead and wounded. Movement in any direction was very difficult.

All the while the French were firing at them from behind the cover of their log wall.[99]

The French had made plans to maintain a heavy volume of fire from their defense line. The most accurate marksmen were posted on the wall, and others were stationed behind to continually receive the recently fired muskets and to pass forward reloaded ones.[100] Extra powder, musket balls, and flints were stored beside the line, along with rocks and hand grenades to throw over the wall if the enemy got too close. Soldiers were even designated to supply pails of drinking water to the overheated men firing along the wall.[101]

After two hours of battle, General Lyman's division was ordered to support the regulars. Up to that time, Timothy and his men would have been a witness to the tense situation, as bloody and mangled wounded were helped to the rear. Now it was their turn. The men needed to keep their formation straight and close the gaps in their lines as they negotiated the wooded terrain. As they exited the forest, Timothy and his men saw the white smoke drifting across the area. The red uniforms of the dead were starkly contrasted against the green needles of the felled trees. The screams of the wounded, and the yells of frustrated men unable to move to their aid, filled the air. Some soldiers were still trying to advance through the hailstorms of lead from the French line, but most were hunched down behind stumps, limbs, or whatever cover they could find. The regular troops were ordered to withdraw, and Timothy's regiment tried to cover their retreat. They could not advance, so they lay or sat behind whatever cover was available. Bullets struck the tree limbs and ground all around them. Those that fired did so rapidly, merely pointing their muskets in the general direction of the enemy because the onslaught of enemy fire was too massive to allow time to actually take aim. Timothy must have been frustrated and scared. There was nothing else for them to do but sit tight, to try to survive.[102] From his position, Timothy witnessed the last tragic attack of the Highlander regiment. This large regiment of over one thousand stubborn warriors refused to withdraw right away. Wounded Scotsmen declined help, and urged their comrades to keep attacking. Some were seen hacking the impeding branches with their huge swords. Some even made it all the way over the log wall, only to be bayoneted there by French grenadiers hurriedly sent to thwart the determined Scots. The near-suicidal tactics of the Forty-second Regiment earned them a deserved reputation for bravery, but it came at a grave cost. In one afternoon this regiment alone lost more than half its men—killed, wounded, or missing.[103]

Abercromby finally accepted defeat around five in the afternoon and ordered a complete withdrawal back down the lake. Whiting's regiment helped to cover the retreat, which ultimately deteriorated into a confused affair. The wounded mixed with the regulars as they all clogged the one small road leading back to the lake. Timothy's company suffered another long night without proper rest. Eventually, they withdrew in the dark. As they made their way, they passed abandoned provisions and equipment. Fires set to consume abandoned supplies lit their route as they continued to trudge back to Lake George.[104] One of the regiment's companies did not get the order to withdraw in the confusion and was left alone for a time, but they fortunately rejoined the regiment at dawn.[105] Once the regiment was reunited, they climbed back into their boats and pushed off into the sparkling water. The men could hardly keep their eyes open as they rowed silently south. The rhythmic squeak of the oars was overpowering and constant all day. The melancholy atmosphere was a stark change from that of their journey on the lake just four days ago.

Timothy's men were totally spent by the time they reached the ruins of Fort William Henry. They had endured so much in the last five days, and yet they were luckier than many of the other regiments. They camped on the east side of the lake and enjoyed staying in one place for four days.[106] After letting the regiment recuperate a bit, Colonel Whiting decided to reestablish a military routine on July 11. The men were ordered into formation twice a day, and Timothy would have made sure their weapons were inspected. They kept busy cleaning the camp and themselves, but surely they all felt low.[107] Dysentery and other health problems increased. Abercromby ordered all sorts of projects to keep the army busy. One especially unpopular order involved having regiments strike their tents and then set them up again in another area of the camp. Timothy's regiment was required to do this on two separate occasions, on the fourteenth and again on the eighteenth. It must have been frustrating to see the men perform this useless exercise. Surely they were relieved when the order to move camp again on the twentieth was rescinded.[108] Timothy's regiment also cleared the land of trees, which was back-breaking labor.[109] The trees were cut down with axes, and then the branches were cut off by teams of men with saws. The trunks were latched onto teams of oxen when they were available, or teams of men when they were not, and they were then dragged away. Another party of men removed the stumps. They dug around the stump until the roots were exposed enough to cut with axes. Then the stump was fastened to iron tackles, and twenty men would haul on ropes to pull it out of the ground. Through this process about forty men could clear about twenty stumps in one laborious day.[110]

The army's faith in Abercromby dissolved.[111] These feelings were shared by the provincials, and the regulars. Many of the provincial officers could not believe they had been ordered to withdraw from Ticonderoga. They complained among themselves that it was unthinkable not to have proceeded with the enterprise when they had plenty of artillery to blast the French defenses and still maintained the advantage of numbers. It was clear that even with the massive English losses of the failed assault on July 8, the French had still been at a disadvantage. Many of the regular officers concurred and complained about Abercromby as well. Timothy heard his men curse Abercromby around the campfires at night. The provincials' new nickname for Abercromby, Mrs. Nabbycrombie, became quite popular among the troops.[112] One man deserted on July 15, the only one in Timothy's company to do so during the campaign.[113] The many frustrated did talk about deserting, but Timothy and the other company officers were able to keep the rest of the company together during these very trying times.

Timothy's company escaped guard duty and construction projects early in August when they went on a scout. Major Rogers led 530 men collected from the provincials, Rangers, and light infantry of the Eightieth Regiment. On August 8, members of Timothy's company were in the advance group of the scout, under the command of Major Israel Putnam, a well-respected ranger from Connecticut.[114] As they advanced along an Indian path in the forest, they were ambushed. The enemy rose from cover in an instant, and fired a volley. The men were completely surprised, and ran to avoid the bullets and tomahawks flying around them.[115] The advance party was overrun by the enemy. Major Putnam was captured, and an Indian tied him to a tree as a prisoner and left him there to resume fighting. Timothy's company soon recovered and fought back fiercely with the Rangers and the regulars. Every fallen log or standing tree provided cover as the enemies maneuvered through the forest. They drove the French and their Indian allies back beyond the point where poor Putnam was tied to a tree; for about an hour the battle raged around him. The lead balls from both sides slammed into the tree to which Putnam was fastened, even passing through portions of his clothing.[116] Timothy's men were in the thick of the musket fire. Their sweat would have soaked their clothes. Grains of foul-tasting powder entered their mouths as they quickly ripped open each paper cartridge with their teeth. The men primed the pans of their muskets as quickly as possible from the cartridges and probably spilled black powder grains all over in their haste. They rammed the powder, paper, and ball down the burning hot barrels of the muskets, and then slid the ramrod back down the groove in the wooden stock. When finally loaded, they scanned the smoke-laden undergrowth for the enemy, unable to distinguish a clear target most of the time. The leaves near them were ripped with enemy musket balls nearly missing their mark, and they returned the fire as best they could.[117]

Finally the French withdrew, and the smoke slowly cleared. The men called to one another to reunite the separated members of the company after the confusing battle. The exhausted men staggered through the woods searching for casualties and further signs of the enemy. Gershom Rowley's shock and amazement grew as he fingered bullet hole after bullet hole in his clothes. He discovered a total of nine, yet he was unharmed.[118] They found Peter Wooster, member of a different company in the Second Connecticut Regiment, among the trees—still alive, though suffering from eleven wounds, eight from musket balls and three from ax blows.[119] Major Putnam was not found and was listed as missing (he would ultimately survive his captivity and return to military service). It was imperative that they finish collecting everyone quickly so that they could get the wounded to the closest care station, Fort Edward, which was a distant fourteen miles away. With cut branches, extra muskets, and blankets, they made crude stretchers to carry the wounded, and set off, marching all night.[120] The moans of the wounded surely drove them to continue despite their physical exhaustion. Many of the badly injured did not last the night, completing the journey only to be buried at the fort's expanding graveyard. The men in Timothy's company had tales of survival to share when they rejoined the regiment. Yet August 8 became a milestone date for the company, when Corporal Ephram Tiffany died, the first of six of the company who would not return that year.[121] The troops' extreme efforts were acknowledged by Colonel Whiting, who noted in the regimental record book that the general had thanked the officers and men on the scout and praised them for their good behavior.[122]

By the afternoon of August 13, Timothy was overseeing the preparations for another scout. He and his men prepared provisions for seven days and checked their equipment.[123] Major Spencer chose his now very experienced Ensign Percival to help him lead ninety-six men from the Second Connecticut Regiment.[124] They rose before dawn on the fourteenth, filled their canteens, pulled their knapsacks and blanket rolls over their shoulders, and lined up for inspection. Timothy oversaw the two sergeants and one corporal checking the men's equipment, making sure they all had musket balls, powder, and water. The other units they would join on this scout made the same preparations in the limited dawn light. Finally they formed into a column and marched out of camp at five o'clock under the overall command of General Lyman. Seven exhausting, sweaty days later, they returned to the monotonous jobs of guard duty and construction.[125]

While Timothy remained in the Lake George area, Lieutenant Colonel Bradstreet led a force of three thousand men west to attack the French Fort Frontenac, which guarded the entrance to the Saint Lawrence River on the eastern shore of Lake Ontario. On August 28, Timothy's company received confirmation that General Amherst's army had captured the French fortress of Louisbourg. This was a great victory for the English since Louisbourg guarded the Atlantic exit of the Saint Lawrence River. Timothy assembled his men along the edge of camp with the rest of the army. The giant ring of soldiers fired sixty-three cannon and three volleys from their muskets in celebration.[126] News soon followed of Bradstreet's successful raid that destroyed Fort Frontenac and the small fleet of enemy ships harbored there. The men at Lake George talked of the possibility of renewing the advance north. Their conversations around the campfires were fueled by rumors and the aspiration that Amherst's army and Bradstreet's force would soon join forces with them so that an advance could indeed be undertaken. Their hopes were dashed by the weather, however. By the time Bradstreet returned to Lake George on September 26, the camp was covered by a thin layer of snow.

As the nights became colder, Timothy and his men lost interest in a further advance. Staying warm became their prime concern. Early in the mornings the men would frantically try to start fires to warm themselves. Their numb, fumbling fingers would strike flint against steel, each spark caressed by their breath into a flame. Timothy obviously thought of Mary and the warm hearth at home. As autumn progressed, the army experienced desertions and near mutinies. Some of the freezing and hungry men grew short-tempered and abandoned military discipline. During this period, Timothy experienced one of the other responsibilities of being an officer, as he took part in a court-martial hearing to deal with infractions of discipline.[127] The rules and practices of the regular army oversaw the lives of all in camp. The soldiers witnessed floggings, hangings, or other forms of corporal punishment almost every day.[128] The men in Timothy's company grew more restless, more aggravated. Three men in the company died in October, further dampening their spirits.[129] Timothy surely longed to follow as he watched the Fourth Connecticut Regiment march toward Fort Edward on October 18. Three more regiments continued the exodus on the twenty-third; by the twenty-fifth, only two regular regiments and the First and Second Connecticut were left at Lake George.[130] Timothy's men had spent the last few days preparing for the winter that was fast approaching. Boats were sunk in the lake to better preserve them during the upcoming harsh weather. They would be raised next year in the spring. More boats were hidden in the woods, and other equipment and supplies were buried. On the evening of the twenty-fourth, temporary huts and rubbish were burned in an enormous fire that bathed the entire camp in light. Timothy must have watched the inferno in jubilation, as they were scheduled to leave the next day.[131] The morning of the twenty-fifth was cold and cloudy, and Timothy's company prepared to leave, but disappointment struck again, as their departure was delayed due to a lack of transport.[132] That night they glumly shivered around their fires, as it snowed. Soon, enough draft animals and wagons were brought up to the lake, and the regiment started the slow march to Fort Edward.

The road between Lake George and Fort Edward is only fourteen miles long, but they spent at least five days moving back and forth on that road, their progress slowed by the heavy cannon, boats, and laden wagons that they pushed and dragged.[133] The weather alternated between rain and snow most days, turning the road into a rutted mass of freezing mud. Timothy's feet would have been wet and cold every day. The regiment spent the first four days of November at Fort Edward cutting trees and clearing roads. After completing these duties, the men received rations of rum on the evening of the fourth, which surely helped warm them as they huddled around fires and dreamed of home.[134] The regiment finally received orders to leave Fort Edward the next morning, and the men could hardly wait. The long journey home for Timothy was finally completed by November 18.[135]

In December, as Timothy was getting used to being home with Mary again, news arrived of another English victory. General John Forbes's force of regulars and provincials had captured Fort Duquesne on November 25. The loss of this strategic fort weakened the French influence with the Indian tribes along the Ohio River Valley, marking a shift in Indian support away from the French—a significant development. From Timothy's vantage it appeared that the crisis was over, that the war was finally turning against the French.

CHAPTER 4

Hopeful Finish

The Connecticut Assembly authorized four regiments to be raised in March 1759 for the upcoming campaign. Wages were increased for the soldiers and more bounties and other inducements were included to attract volunteers,[136] but Timothy showed no interest this year. Over the four and a half years of his marriage to Mary, he had been away on three campaigns and had been called up for the August 1757 alarm. So it was probably due to his family obligations and his longing to stay with loved ones that Timothy decided not to serve in the company Joseph Spencer was raising in 1759. Spencer had been promoted to lieutenant colonel of the Second Connecticut Regiment,[137] and he tried to collect veterans from the past campaign for his company. Israel Harding, who had been at the rank of second lieutenant the year before, was now first lieutenant. James Sparrow was sergeant again, and William Akens and Abner Scovel returned as corporals.[138] Corporal Gershom Rowley, the lucky survivor of the fierce skirmish in August 1758, did not tempt fate again in 1759. Gershom had married Mary Curtis on December 14, 1757, and he stayed home as well. The list of veterans from 1758 was small. The company had over one hundred men, but Spencer had commanded only twenty-seven of them the previous year. Fortunately, one of the other sergeants and over thirty privates had served in a campaign before 1758, so over half of Spencer's men were at least veterans.[139]

Timothy probably wished the men in Spencer's company well as they left that spring, then awaited news of the campaign as he attended to the many tasks on the family farm that summer. The Second Connecticut Regiment marched over the same wet, mosquito-infested ground in June and July as they had in 1758. Their routine was the same as the year before, now under the command of General Amherst, the victorious commander of last year's capture of Louisbourg. Late in the summer, Timothy would have heard that Fort Carillon, at Ticonderoga, had been captured easily, after the French had blown it up and retreated. Fort St. Frederic, at Crown Point, fell soon thereafter—the French having again withdrawn without making a stand. News of English victories continued as the year advanced. Fort Niagara, near the western end of Lake Ontario, fell, and even Quebec City, the capital of French Canada, was captured after a long and dramatic siege. General Wolfe and General Montcalm, commanders of the opposing armies at Quebec, both died from battle wounds just days before the French surrendered the city.

After the harvests had been collected in East Haddam, the men in Spencer's company finally came home and shared their experiences in warm taverns over well-earned drinks. The men enjoyed their acclaim but also expressed much dissatisfaction with the campaign. Timothy learned that the provincials had spent most of their time building or reinforcing fortifications and roads. Their provisions had proved less than promised, and the men's health had waned during the autumn. Of course, no one had to explain this plight to Timothy; he had experienced it all himself.

As another cold New England winter held its grip on the land, the people in East Haddam discussed the upcoming campaign. Montreal was the last stronghold remaining in French Canada, and General Amherst meant to capture it. That one last campaign seemed to promise victory. The financial strain of the last five years of war had forced the Colony of Connecticut to raise taxes,[140] which had lain heavily on all landowners. Connecticut would spend over 1.2 million pounds on the war effort, yet England did not follow through and only reimbursed the colony for a quarter of those expenses.[141] The people needed an end to the war, and Timothy got caught up in the emotional fervor to serve this purpose. The six pounds pay he would earn each month as an officer[142] would help finance his own family farm, six pounds being enough to purchase about six hogs.[143] Timothy accepted the nomination to be second lieutenant in Joseph Spencer's company. Spencer was nominated to be lieutenant colonel of the Second Connecticut Regiment again. Since Spencer was to be the second-in-command of the regiment and have duties that would take him away from the command of the company, he was fortunate to have an experienced officer like Timothy to help command the company. The first lieutenant, Levis Wells, did not have as much campaign experience, so Timothy, along with James Sparrow as ensign, would be the officers Spencer could turn to during the trials ahead.[144] Timothy had worked with Sparrow as a sergeant in 1758 and knew Sparrow had been with Spencer the year before; importantly, the three of them already had a working relationship. In fact, most of the men in the company were experienced. Of the eighty-three men under the officers, three sergeants, two corporals, and fifty-three privates had served in a previous campaign.[145] They were lucky to raise the men they did, for the Colony of Connecticut overall had trouble recruiting in 1760. Only 3,229 men answered the call, far below the five thousand requested.[146] Colonel Whiting would command their regiment again,[147] and they were ordered to assemble with the other three Connecticut regiments at Albany.

Two men deserted from the company on May 25,[148] before the campaign commenced. Timothy was able to keep the rest of the company together, and no further desertions occurred in his company for the remainder of the campaign. Witnessing five hundred lashes imposed on a deserter from the regiment on June 17 may have helped to deter the men. Jerimiah Hastings's[149] body shook each time the lash struck his bloody back, adding new cuts to his skin. The stern disciplinary actions of the regular army were part of their daily lives again.

General Amherst planned a three-pronged attack on Montreal. The regular troops at Quebec City would advance up the Saint Lawrence River, supported by naval ships. Another force of regulars and provincials would advance from Crown Point on Lake Champlain and down the Richelieu River. Meanwhile Amherst, with the largest army, would advance west from Albany, up the Mohawk River, across Lake Oneida, down the Oneida River to Lake Ontario and from there down the Saint Lawrence River. It was a complicated plan to trap the French forces at Montreal, requiring all three groups to arrive in Montreal at nearly the same moment. And there was the overarching risk that any one of the three English forces might be defeated before the other two could come to its aid. All four Connecticut regiments, under the command of General Lyman, would accompany Amherst's army.

From the end of May until June 19, the Connecticut men assembled outside of Albany. That year Albany was suffering from an outbreak of smallpox, and entrance to the town was restricted.[150] Smallpox was a horrible disease that ravaged communities during the eighteenth century. Highly contagious, it was transmitted through contact with infected people or infected items such as bed linens or clothes. The visible signs of the disease were pimples on the skin that would grow into pustules, like large blisters. These would eventually dry and flake off, leaving scars, called pockmarks. The infection lasted about four weeks, if the individual survived. Around 30 percent of those infected died. Smallpox killed millions during the eighteenth century, including entire Indian communities in North America.[151] Everyone was justly frightened of the disease.

Timothy avoided Albany, and occupied his company with the ordeal of moving bateaux, equipment, and supplies. Each regiment was assigned a certain number of wagons and bateaux for transporting themselves and their provisions. Not only did Timothy oversee the handling and loading of the wagons and bateaux of his company, he also had to make sure both the men and camp were kept clean. General Lyman was strict about hygiene for the prevention of disease; his orders included such details as requiring the men to wear stockings and shoes in camp.[152]

Finally all the Connecticut troops arrived, and they were ordered to leave their camps near Albany. Early on the morning of June 20, Timothy's company received three days' rations and started the march west.[153] This was new territory for Timothy and for many of the men who had served north of Albany in the past. While some in the regiment rowed the boats up the Mohawk River, the rest marched on the road along the bank of the waterway. They followed the Forty-second Highland Regiment, which could easily have reminded Timothy of that horrible July 8 in 1758 when so many of them were slaughtered attacking the French at Ticonderoga. The Forty-second had received new recruits and looked as tough as it had on the eve of that fateful day. They all arrived at Schenectady on the morning of June 22.[154]

Amherst was constantly concerned that he was falling behind his timetable. It was taking longer than anticipated to move everything. So he proceeded west from Schenectady to learn of the delays firsthand and urged General Lyman and the Connecticut men to transport the remainder of the army's watercraft and provisions to Lake Ontario. The march up the Mohawk River continued at daybreak on June 24.[155] The process was slow, and the difficult march probably left painful memories in the minds of the men. There were few settlements along the river until they reached Fort Hunter where Schoharie Creek joined the Mohawk River. Fort Hunter was, in essence, four wooden blockhouses connected by wooden walls and, therefore, only defensible against raiding Indians, as one cannonball could easily smash the walls into splinters.

This was the land of the Mohawk members of the Iroquois Confederacy. Across the creek from the fort was a Mohawk village, the first Timothy would ever have seen. Its log palisade enclosed longhouse dwellings. The longhouses varied in length from thirty to over one hundred feet and were about twenty feet wide. They were covered with layers of elm bark laid on a frame of bent saplings, and their roofs were punctured by smoke holes placed directly above the fire pits inside.[156] The Iroquois Confederacy was now an ally to the English, but Timothy may still have been uneasy moving among the Indians, for it was common knowledge that many Iroquois remained allied to the French, and one could never know which way their loyalty might shift. Recent reports[157] of Indian attacks further up the Mohawk River added to the uncertainty.

West of Fort Hunter, for eighteen miles along the river, the ground was fertile, and Timothy and his men passed many individual frontier farmhouses. West of Fort Herkimer, the Mohawk River became narrow and shallow, slowing the progress of the bateaux even more. The road in this section became very difficult as well. Many of the small bridges were washed out and needed repair. The rutted and muddy tracks were almost impassable for the wagons.[158] Each tedious mile further up the river drew them closer to Fort Stanwix where they would finally leave the Mohawk and carry the bateaux overland four miles to Wood Creek—a driving goal for the men because there the struggle upstream would end, as Wood Creek flowed west to Lake Oneida.

Fort Stanwix was a wood and earthen structure with four bastions connected by curtain walls. The bastions formed the four corners, and protruded so that cannon fire could be directed at the approaches to the curtain walls. This strong fort rested on a rise of land between the Mohawk River and Wood Creek known as the Oneida Carrying Place. The provincials surely celebrated their arrival at Fort Stanwix, but their exuberance did not last. The men were disappointed to find that Wood Creek was exceedingly shallow due to a lack of rain. An Indian birch-bark canoe could maneuver in such shallows, but the fully loaded bateaux had to be pushed and pulled by the Connecticut men walking alongside in the creek. Fallen trees blocked their passage as well,[159] and the men had to lift the bateaux by hand over these impediments or clear a passage with axes. Their dreams of rowing easily downstream with the current were deterred until they approached Lake Oneida where the depth of the water increased.

This was the domain of the Oneida Indians, also part of the Iroquois Confederacy. Oneida Lake is over twenty miles long and over five miles wide in the middle. It was surrounded by forest, but for the first time since Timothy had left Schenectady his view was not limited by the thick woods. It was a beautiful sight to behold, and could easily have reminded Timothy of the views of Long Island Sound from the Connecticut shoreline. The crossing of Oneida Lake and journey down the Oneida River were relatively easy. The men avoided the falls on the Oswego River with a sixty-yard portage around them. Fortunately the bateaux did not have to be carried because members of the army ahead of them had left wooden rollers at the portage, allowing the craft to be pushed over land and saving vital time and effort. After the falls, the river was rapid, accelerating their voyage but causing many accidents with rocks and tree limbs. Many of their bateaux incurred damages.[160] Finally, on July 22, they arrived at Lake Ontario. Timothy was probably stunned by the immense size of this inland sea. He could not see the far shore even on the clearest day. Timothy's company had spent over a month marching and hauling their bateaux and provisions to get to this assembly point for Amherst's army. Beyond here, they would be entering enemy territory.

The army camped around the rebuilt Fort Oswego, which had been destroyed by the French in 1756. A new and larger Fort Ontario was being built across the river. This fort had been placed on a rise above the river and the lake, generally on a much better site from which to defend this outpost. Amherst was determined to strengthen and protect the supply route of the army on this campaign. As the regiments gathered along the lake, they were put right to work, busily building up the fortifications and repairing the damaged bateaux.

Sir William Johnson led the group of Iroquois Indians accompanying him into the camp on July 23.[161] There were hundreds of them, dressed in colorful, multifarious attire. Timothy would not have seen so many Indians since the Battle of Lake George in 1755. It was hard to fathom that so many were now willing to fight with the English, definitely a sign of the changing fortunes of the antagonists in this war.

A heavy storm hit the camp on the twenty-fourth. Lighting slashed through the sky and cracked the air. Thunder reverberated across Lake Ontario and wind forcefully flapped the white canvas tents. Rain drenched the entire camp and caused the lake to suddenly rise sixteen inches. Vessels that had been carefully stored on the shore were found floating about, and men had to splash through the rising water to drag them back inland.[162] It was almost as if the earth was sounding its own tumult to join the war drums of the Indians camped near the army. The storm slowed the progress of much of the army's work, but not for long. Carpenters repaired the damaged bateaux. Others constructed Fort Ontario in shifts, day and night.[163] The ever-mounting casks of provisions had to be organized and checked for damage and spoilage. Larger craft were assembled to carry the heavy twelve-pound cannon. Overall, decisions were made as to what equipment would be essential for the next part of the journey and what would be left behind.

Timothy would have noticed two vessels approaching camp on July 27. These were the *Apollo* and the *Mohawk*, commanded by Captain Loring of the Royal Navy. They had been constructed at Fort Niagara, at the western end of the lake, with the mission of protecting the army from the French ships there. The *Apollo* had two masts with square sails and a trysail set behind the mainmast.[164] It carried four nine-pound guns, fourteen six-pound guns, and one hundred seamen. The *Mohawk* was rigged the same way but had sixteen six-pound guns and ninety seamen.[165] The French schooner, *Iroquoise*, and brig, the *Outaouaise*, each of ten guns,[166] had been observed on the lake before Timothy arrived. Captain Loring had been ordered to intercept and attempt to destroy the French ships, but with the return of Loring's ships came news that the French had probably escaped down the Saint Lawrence River.[167] The *Iroquoise* and the *Outaouaise* therefore remained a threat to the army's proposed advance on the water.

During the evening of July 29, a confrontation between some of the allied Indians and the English disrupted the camp. Fortunately, William Johnson was able to put a stop to the conflict before any real harm was done.[168] The uneasy alliance held, but while the two very different cultures resided together, the potential for discord was always present. Amherst's army was made up of a varied sort. The number of Indians ranged, during the course of the campaign, from about five hundred to over one thousand. There were two companies of Rangers, a regiment from New Jersey, three from New York, and the four from Connecticut. Even the regular regiments included a rainbow of backgrounds. The Forty-second and Seventy-seventh were recruited from Scotland. The Forty-fourth, Forty-sixth, Fifty-fifth, and Eightieth regiments contained men from all over the British Isles and North America.[169] While the Sixtieth Royal Americans regiment was primarily recruited from North America, it included men of German and Swiss ancestry.[170] This diverse collection grew in size through early August to nearly eleven thousand men.[171] With the exception of the Indians, the men were held together by the bond of army discipline. Timothy was reminded of this association on July 30 when one man was hanged for desertion. Ten men were sentenced to death overall, but nine were pardoned by General Amherst. The tenth faced his sentence alone, as he had been a repeat offender.[172] The sight of his slowly twisting body suspended in the air by a rope served as a dramatic reminder of Amherst's authority.

In an effort to placate their Indian allies, Amherst ordered a celebration of sorts on August 1. The *Apollo* was re-christened the *Onondaga*, the name of one of the important tribes in the Iroquois Confederacy. A large flag with an image of an Onondaga warrior was hoisted on the ship, and regiments fired volleys while one cannon in the fort roared a salute. The guns on the *Onondaga* responded in kind, and the Indian chiefs were given punch to drink. After the festivities, Amherst increased the number of men working on the fort.[173] He was planning to advance soon, and he hoped to complete as much work on Fort Ontario as possible while the men of his army were available.

The number of Indians with the army continued to grow; by August 5 there were over 1,300 around the camp. The Indians had turned the preparation and assembly for war into a family gathering and celebration. Ritualized meetings of distant clan members continued for days, and fireside celebrations lasted into the nights. Over half of those in attendance were actually women and children whom Johnson tried to send home as quickly as possible, as the army was scheduled to finally move.[174]

On August 6, Amherst ordered the *Onondaga* and the *Mohawk* to move forward accompanied by a collection of Rangers, light infantry, grenadiers, and highlanders following in smaller boats as an advance guard. Timothy and his men spent the next few days organizing the provisions that the company would take with them and ensuring that the bateaux they would use were adequately repaired and fit for travel on Lake Ontario, which was renowned for its strong winds and rough waters. The advance guard sent back word that they had indeed encountered those winds and some of their craft had already been lost. As a result, a large quantity of food provisions was destroyed, and nine thousand musket cartridges were spoiled. On August 9 Timothy's company received its orders to load provisions into the vessels and prepare for departure the following day. The army cleaned the camp while officers completed a court-martial trial, resulting in the execution of four condemned men that evening.[175]

As the sun peeked through the trees on the horizon, the drums sounded, and the army scurried to break down its tents and finish loading the bateaux. The large fleet of varied craft embarked on the sparkling lake. The plan was for the light infantry to advance in front, the Indians and artillery to form the right column, with the regulars in the center and the provincials at the left. Some of the army traveled about thirty miles that day before the wind grew dangerous and forced them to find shelter along the shore.[176] High winds forced the bateaux to rock aggressively in the high waves, and cold spray hit the men's faces and obscured their vision as they struggled with the oars. Each huge wave threatened to overturn the bateaux. The forceful gales pushed the wooden vessels ever closer together, making it difficult to row as oars from different boats collided. The bateaux became more difficult to steer without the forward momentum caused by men constantly pulling the oars, and the craft would fall victim to the whims of the driving wind. The potential of serious collisions between the small craft threatened the supplies and lives of the men as they were pushed up and then rolled down with each swell. To avoid further loss they were ordered back to Fort Ontario.[177]

The fierce winds continued well into the morning of the next day, and the divided army did not reunite until the thirteenth. It had been an inauspicious beginning. Some men even suffered from seasickness—so great had been the power of the Ontario's waters. And provisions and ammunition were dampened and spoiled by the stormy water. Needless to say, Amherst's timetable was delayed by the need to reorganize, restock, and repair many of the bateaux. Rain all through the night of the fourteenth further stalled the distribution of provisions, retarding the army's departure the next day and frustrating Amherst. The maze of islands the men encountered at the beginning of the Saint Lawrence River slowed the pace further. The small bateaux could navigate any of the adjoining channels, but deeper channels had to be found for the *Onondaga* and *Mohawk*. Also a consideration was the fact that the larger vessels were needed for the protection of the smaller craft, especially given that the French schooner *Iroquoise* and the brig *Outaouaise* were still somewhere ahead of them. Despite this concern, when one of the English ships ran aground, Amherst made the decision to proceed without the larger ships in an effort to hasten the advance. The English had five row galleys larger than the bateaux armed with four twelve-pound guns and one howitzer. Amherst hoped these would be enough.[178]

On the seventeenth of August, the army discovered the French vessel *Outaouaise* trying to sail upriver to attack the bateaux, but calm wind restricted the brig's movement. The English row galleys moved in to attack. The French ship had ten cannon and four small swivel guns, but its advantage in firepower was negated because the row galleys were not restricted by the lack of wind, and could maneuver to positions where the French could not bring all their guns to bear. Still, the cannon duel lasted two or three hours. The French fired over one hundred shots, while the nimble row galleys returned seventy-two blasts of cannon. The French were finally forced to strike their colors because they were suffering extensive casualties and could not escape due to the still air. French prisoners were taken to shore, and men were put to work repairing the captured vessel. Amherst refused to lose any more time and pushed his army downriver eight more miles before stopping to camp. He was approaching the French Fort Levis, and he was eager to attack it. Even the heavy rain that night did not deter Amherst. On August 18, he ordered the regulars to advance on Fort Levis, which was situated on an island in the middle of the river. The move would be risky because the soldiers would have to row their bateaux toward the island while exposed to the guns in the fort, and they had only four of the row galleys operating at that point to provide covering fire.[179]

Fort Levis had just been finished that summer. Captain Pierre Pouchot had been assigned there in March and had worked his small garrison feverishly to turn the island into a respectable fortification. Pouchot was a regular French army

COMMON COURAGE

officer with experience in defending fortifications. His guiding hand was the key, for his resources were very slim. To increase the number of artillery at the fort, even damaged cannon barrels were used in makeshift emplacements. Wood-supported earthen walls provided the fort's main protection. But even earth was in short supply on the island, and it had to be dredged from the riverbed and brought in on boats from the shorelines. By the time Amherst's army arrived, Pouchot and his tiny garrison of less than three hundred were prepared to delay the English army for as long as possible.[180]

Amherst sent his soldiers downstream on both sides of the fort and established positions on the other islands close to Fort Levis and along the shore. Of course, there were casualties from the French fire as the bateaux moved on the river, but the first step of the siege was complete. For the next seven days the regulars and provincials dug earthworks on the islands and shore surrounding the fort.[181]

Timothy spent the siege camped at the settlement of La Gallette (sometimes called La Presentation), upriver from Fort Levis. The French had tried to destroy the village and wooden stockade fort there before the arrival of the English, but they had only succeeded in demolishing the roofs of the houses. Nearby, abandoned fields were full of ripe corn, beans, and squash which were greatly appreciated by the men in Timothy's regiment—a welcome change of diet from the regular rations of dried peas and salt pork.

Overall, the charge of Whiting's regiment was to protect the rear of the army and to forward equipment and supplies to the siege. While performing guard duty and organizing supplies, Timothy would have heard the constant pounding of the cannon around Fort Levis. At night, the flashes of fire silhouetted the tall pine trees along the Saint Lawrence River, making sleep a precious rarity. Timothy's regiment also kept watch on the eighty French prisoners captured in the action against the brig *Outaouaise*.[182] While at La Gallette, Colonel Whiting would frequently dine with Captain La Broquerie of the *Outaouaise*.[183] And it is possible that Joseph Spencer and even Timothy were included in these meals, as it was the custom of the period for officers to eat together.

Whenever the soldiers remained in one camp for a few days they would fill their free time playing cards, listening to fiddle music, singing hymns, reading the Bible, or carving inscriptions and pictures on their powder horns. While at La Gallette, Richardson Minor artfully carved his powder horn. Minor was a trained silversmith and clockmaker from Stratford, Connecticut, who had been made the regimental armorer for Whiting's Second Connecticut expressly because of his skills as a metalworker. If Timothy had to check on any repairs of weapons while at La Gallette, he may also have admired Minor's progress on his powder horn. Minor carved his name in precise bold letters and meticulously framed it with stylized tulips. Some soldiers had their horns carved by others. Colonel Whiting's horn had been carved in 1756 by John Bush, an African-American craftsman who is credited with a number of admirable carvings. John Tribble in Timothy's company also had a beautifully decorated horn complete with the playful inscription: "Don't take this horn for fear of shame for on it stands ye owner's name." Joseph Spencer's son, Hobart, also in Timothy's company, had on his horn drawings of soldiers in formation performing the firing drill, as well as pictures of mounted troops firing their pistols. His inscription read: "Men of might they take delight in gun and sword that they may fight."[184] Around the campfires at night, the men in Timothy's company probably shared stories about the artwork on their horns along with many other aspects of the campaign, all the while likely harboring deep fears of what lay ahead.

On the twenty-third of August, Amherst ordered an assault on Fort Levis. He had numerous cannon ring the fort, and with the repaired captured French vessel the *Outaouaise*, renamed the *Williamson*,[185] he now had three armed sailing ships to support the attack. The other French vessel, the *Iroquoise*, had been scuttled since it could not escape downstream through the rapids, making the small garrison of Fort Levis all they had left with which to oppose the English. Amherst collected six companies of grenadiers, the best and most hardened soldiers in each regular regiment, to lead the assault with the light infantry. They positioned themselves in bateaux and waited for the signal to row quickly toward the island fort.[186]

The afternoon assault began with a heavy barrage of cannon fire in an attempt to eliminate, or at least suppress, the opposing French cannon in the fort. The *Mohawk*, the *Onondaga*, and the *Williamson* moved into position close to the fort and dropped anchors to hold themselves in position against the river's current. They then added their cannon fire to the pounding of Fort Levis. The French, under Pouchot, returned the fire, the roar of guns echoing throughout the forest. Under constant attack, the French bravely retaliated by concentrating their cannon fire on the three ships. The *Mohawk* suffered first when a cannonball smashed into a plank on the hull, causing water to rush in below deck. The ship's commander cut the anchor cable and let the vessel drift downstream out of range of the French guns so that repairs could be made. The next to accompany the *Mohawk* was the *Williamson* when a lucky shot sliced her anchor cable, and the current carried her out of the fight. The *Onondaga* then faced the French cannon fire alone. Pouchot's artillery kept up such a rapid fire that Captain Loring of the *Onondaga* soon gave up and attempted to drift to safety as well. His luck ran out, however, and the ship ran aground close to the fort. Loring had to surrender the *Onondaga* to Pouchot. The cannon duel continued, but Amherst was forced to accept that his plans had been defeated by the Frenchmen's furious retaliatory fire, and he cancelled the assault.[187]

Still the cannonade of the fort went on, day and night. Even rain on the twenty-fourth did not stop the artillery. Gradually the earthworks at Fort Levis collapsed from the impact of the incessant English fire. Finally, on the afternoon of August 25, an English flag was raised over the shattered defenses of the fort to signal that Pouchot was finally ready to ask for terms of surrender.[188] Only then did the artillery stop. The silence was understood as a sure sign of victory, and that evening the English celebrated around their campfires.

The next day Amherst ordered the army to clean up the area of the siege and to start repairing Fort Levis for English usage. This work continued through August 30 along with efforts to raise the scuttled French schooner, the *Iroquoise*. This vessel would become a valuable addition to the English flotilla on Lake Ontario. The soldiers had spent many days digging the trenches and earthworks around the fort for the siege. Now, they bent their backs again, tearing down those same earthworks and filling in the trenches to deter any enemy force that might try to recapture the fort.

On the twenty-eighth Amherst received news from Indian scouts that the English army advancing from Quebec and the army moving north from Lake Champlain were both approaching Montreal. Amherst was not far from being able to join them but first had to mount one last obstacle—a series of dangerous rapids on the Saint Lawrence River. The army proceeded on the afternoon of August 31 after collecting enough usable bateaux to carry the men and their supplies. At first the rapids were manageable, but before long the river's current strengthened and passage became more precarious. Raging water soon splashed over the sides of the heavily loaded bateaux, a number of which actually overturned. Between rapids, the men busily bailed out the water-laden and battered bateaux. On September 2, a particularly wild rapid drove one of the bateaux into the rocks by the shore, and four men drowned. That night, a violent storm hit the army's encampment along the river. The wind whipped the tents, and the rain drenched everything. It was a miserable night for the men, and the storm continued all morning on September 3. Amherst grew very impatient as the dangerous winds prevented the army from proceeding until the following day.[189]

The army rose before dawn on September 4 so that they could start moving as quickly as possible once the newest set of rapids became visible in the dawn light. These would be the most difficult they had faced, and the unusually high volume of water passing over the rocks added to the danger. Most of the army marched along the shore in an effort to lighten the bateaux and ease the passage, but the swift current would claim many bateaux regardless. The flow carried the wooden craft over boulders and plunged them down into a foaming maelstrom of colliding currents. The oarsmen struggled to keep their fragile craft upright and fought powerful eddies that threatened to spin them off track into obstacles of jagged rocks, fallen trees, or each other. The air was filled with shouts of the bateaux men, the rattling of wooden poles and oars on boulders, and the constant roar of the river. Overturned bateaux, floating casks, and soldiers struggling in the water added to the mounting list of obstacles to avoid. It took two days for the army to pass through this series of rapids, known as the Thicket, the Cascades, and the Hole. In the end, the powerful force of the water had smashed more than fifty watercraft, and eighty-four men perished. Countless supplies and equipment littered the riverbed, including a number of cannon.[190] Timothy lost one man at this time. Ebenezer Chapman, a member of one of the families in his neighborhood in East Haddam, died on September 5. His was the third death in Timothy's company.[191] All told, the rough waters of the Saint Lawrence engulfed more lives in Amherst's army than those lost during the siege of Fort Levis.[192]

Amherst worried about the delay, but the army had survived the natural difficulties and was now within striking distance of Montreal. The shaken bateaux men recovered their wits and whatever equipment could be salvaged. At daybreak on the sixth, the regimental drums woke the men and within half an hour they started rowing on the last leg of their advance. They met little resistance as they landed at the village of Lachine, on the large island of Montreal. Amherst quickly initiated the army's march toward the city. The three New York regiments and two of the Connecticut regiments were left to guard the landing area, while Whiting's and Lyman's Connecticut regiments and the New Jersey regiment marched with the regulars to face the French.[193] They marched nine miles through numerous French settlements. Many of the French had abandoned their homes before the English arrived. Those that remained were quick to submit. Knowing the horrors inflicted on the English by the Indians allied to the French throughout the war, the same was expected in retaliation in this instance. But Amherst maintained control of the Iroquois in his army, and atrocities inflicted on the French were kept to a minimum.[194] The homes that Timothy's regiment passed were reportedly quite clean, complete with framed windowpanes. A number of large villas for the wealthy merchants were spotted, and the men also took notice of the rich earth on the abundant farms.[195] That night they camped outside the city of Montreal on the rise of land northwest of the city.[196] It was an exciting moment for Timothy and the men in his company. The three English armies converging from three separate points of the compass had arrived together and trapped the French army in Montreal. It was an amazingly successful maneuver achieved through the many strenuous efforts of the valiant soldiers.

The next morning the regiments formed into lines facing the French and waited. The provincial regiments stood with the regulars, ready for battle.[197] They had gained a lot of experience in the last six years; they even looked more like the regulars since they donned uniforms now. (Some of the Connecticut men still had red coats with yellow cuffs even though the colony had started issuing blue with red cuffs for this campaign.[198]) General Lyman had worked on the discipline and appearance of the Connecticut troops, both of which were much improved, but they still did not garner the respect of the regular English officers.

From their position on a rise above the city, Timothy would have observed the numerous stone and wooden homes, most no taller than two stories. The spires of three churches, the walls of the Catholic convents, and the towers of the seminary rose distinctly above the houses.[199] Here lay the last main bastion of France in Canada—a thin collection of buildings along the north bank of the Saint Lawrence River. The goal of the entire campaign spread out before them like a banquet table; all they had to do was advance and take a seat.

Amherst sent messages to the commanders of the other two armies, and traveled about, inspecting the French defenses of Montreal. While organizing his next move, he received a message from the French asking for a termination of the hostilities.[200] The French army was a mere skeleton of its former size. Most of the French militia forces had deserted, and their regular regiments were much reduced from the years of campaigning without enough replacements arriving from Europe.[201] Moreover, while the city of Montreal was surrounded by a stone wall and a shallow moat, it could not withstand artillery fire and was thus indefensible. In short, the French were in a desperate situation and unable to retreat.

The ensuing details of the surrender of French territory in Canada were negotiated, and the official surrender ceremony held on September 8. Timothy must have been relieved to have victory come without incurring yet more violence. It was five years to the day since Timothy had first experienced battle on the shore of Lake George, and finally the conquest of French Canada was complete—the men's exhaustive exertions and suffering along the long march from Albany were now worthwhile.

That night, as the men toasted victory around their fires, Timothy enjoyed the company of those who had shared this war with him, many of whom had been with him on previous campaigns. William Markham and Zepheniah Mitchell had accompanied Timothy in Captain Dimock's company in 1755. Together they had all experienced war for the first time. Benjamin Brooks was also there in 1755, but in another company. Zepheniah had also joined with Timothy in Captain Wells's company in 1756. James Sparrow, Nathan Beebe, James Booge, and John Sheparson had all raced with Timothy in August 1757 for the relief of Fort William Henry. There were sixteen who had served in 1758 under Joseph Spencer with Timothy, three of whom had also served with him in an earlier campaign.[202] Gershom Rowley should have been there to share the moment as he had been on every other campaign with Timothy, but he had stayed home for this one. Surely, Timothy longed to be home as well. However, even though French Canada had been conquered, Amherst planned to retain the provincials.[203]

General Lyman received orders on September 10 to take charge of the four Connecticut regiments and return along the route of their advance. Lyman and three regiments were to proceed to Fort Ontario, while Whiting's regiment would march further to Fort Stanwix,[204] where once again they would form a construction corps. The weeks spent there were difficult for the men as they increasingly longed to return home. Managing their discontentment was nearly impossible when officers like Timothy shared that yearning. Adding insult to injury, disease struck again, and nine men in Timothy's company died (out of a total of twelve for the whole campaign).[205] It seemed such a waste for so many to die after the defeat of the French in Canada was complete; thus the gratification of victory that September was overshadowed by sorrow in November. Nonetheless, the final homecoming late in November must have been wonderful. War continued around the globe, but Timothy's involvement had come to a close.

The next year, Connecticut sent two regiments under the command of Lyman and Whiting to serve the war effort. Now that French Canada was conquered, fewer felt a pressing need to join. The Assembly nominated Timothy to serve as a second lieutenant in Whiting's regiment, but he declined. Even Joseph Spencer abstained from service. The two regiments were stationed at Crown Point, along the shore of Lake Champlain, and they labored on the massive fortifications planned to guard the lake. In 1762, two more regiments were raised. The new threat of Spain having joined the war against England inspired some of Timothy's comrades to join Whiting's Second Connecticut Regiment. Levis Wells and James Sparrow served, along with other family members from East Haddam. Fortunately, Whiting's regiment served at Crown Point again. As dull as that station was, it was far better than the experience of Lyman's regiment, which served in the expedition against Spanish Havana, on the island of Cuba. That campaign ended with the successful capture of the important fortified harbor, but at the horrific cost of half of Lyman's regiment.[206] The dreadful tropical heat, spoiled provisions, and unsanitary conditions drained the men, allowing malaria and dysentery to terminate many lives. The war finally ended with a treaty on February 10, 1763.

Timothy and Mary achieved their dream, acquiring a family farm of their own in Chatham, a community just north of East Haddam.[207] Timothy's younger brother, Rowland, was raising his own family there as well.[208] In March 1774, Timothy's father gave parcels of land to his children from his many holdings in East Haddam and Chatham. Both Timothy and Rowland received 100 acres in Chatham from this generous distribution.[209] The combined families were busy. By the early 1770's, Timothy and Mary had three sons and three daughters; Rowland's family had five boys.[210] With so many relatives in East Haddam and Chatham to support one another, the Percivals' life was bountiful, and their future appeared promising. Little did they know, forthcoming developments would alter their lives once again.

CHAPTER 5
War Returns

The battles of Lexington and Concord on April 19, 1775, would mark the reintroduction of armed conflict to New England. It would come as no surprise to colonists like Timothy and Mary, since the political tension had been mounting for years. Land-rich, cash-poor farmers in Connecticut (as elsewhere in the colonies) had suffered under increased taxes designed to pay for the French and Indian War. Victory in that war ignited hopes of financial relief, so when the English Parliament placed new taxes on the colonies during the years following the war, resistance grew. The Percivals, like thousands of others, had made serious monetary and physical sacrifices during the war, and they found it hard to accept more taxes and restrictions placed on them, especially from a government in which they were granted no local representation.

Disagreements with Parliament really augmented with the Proclamation of 1763, which restricted colonial settlement from the vast new land west of the Appalachian Mountains amassed from victory over the French in the recent war. During the preceding two decades, the population of Connecticut had grown from roughly 110,000 to almost 200,000.[211] Accordingly, over that period available farmland had grown increasingly scarce. This was painfully obvious to the Percivals who faced the ever-possible prospect of being unable to divide their land into meaningful parcels for the next generation. Every family farm needed space for crops, not only for human consumption but also for the livestock. Access to wooded lots was essential as well—the heating requirements of a single home could deforest close to a third of an acre every year.[212] Timothy's farm could not support all his children as they started their own families; therefore, they would need to seek land outside Connecticut. The virgin lands of the Ohio River Valley were a logical outlet for the growing American population, yet the 1763 proclamation barred settlement there.

Then in 1764 and 1765, Parliament passed the Revenue, Currency, Stamp, and Quartering acts. The first three raised taxes or impeded colonial trade, and the last required colonists to feed and house British soldiers that were stationed or passing through their vicinity. Colonial economics were based primarily on a system of exchanging goods and services among themselves on credit, so money rarely changed hands. The extra taxes pulled resources out of each community and, therefore, impaired the breadth of exchange and consequent further development of those local resources. The American colonists organized economic boycotts of British goods in response, and forced the repeal of many of the acts, but not before Parliament passed the Declaratory Act of 1766, stating that Parliament had the authority to enact laws for the colonies in all cases whatsoever—thereby virtually stripping the colonists of any de jure means towards resistance in the future.

In 1767, the Townshend Acts added insult to injury by placing duties on paper, glass, lead paint, and tea. Parliament then suspended jurisdiction of the colonial assembly of New York, charging it with refusal to pay debts related to the quartering of British troops. During the ensuing years, other assemblies were suspended, as well, in an effort to weaken the reach and effects of colonial resistance. Despite this effort, colonists effectively enacted more boycotts on British goods, ultimately forcing the repeal of the Townshend Acts duties, except for the one on tea. The political struggle stagnated until tragedy struck on March 5, 1770, when the infamous Boston Massacre of five colonial citizens inflamed passions again. Colonial opposition to the tax on tea reached a head in December 1773, and huge quantities of tea were destroyed by colonists in Boston harbor in protest. Parliament responded by closing the harbor until the citizens paid for the destroyed tea, thereby forcing many Bostonians out of work and cutting off their main supply route.

The idea that their inherent liberties as Englishmen were being infringed was further endorsed by much of the clergy in New England. Passages from the Bible were quoted proclaiming the law of liberty, as in the book of James, 1:25 and 2:12. Also frequently cited was 1 Peter 2:16, which urged believers to live as free men responsible only to God. Some clergy would even speak directly about their political rights as Englishmen. Many sermons espousing these beliefs were printed and distributed throughout New England, so that the clergy's influence spread well beyond individual congregations.[213] The sermon Timothy heard in East Haddam before setting off on the campaign of 1758 is a good example of how important an impact the clergy had in these matters. On May 30, 1758, Pastor Estabrook clearly stated that, "When our lives liberties and properties are directly threatened, and imminently exposed, we may take up arms in our defense." [214] Clearly this charge—ordained from the pulpit—re-emboldened the hearts and minds of already disenchanted New Englanders.

The community of Chatham actively resisted Parliament, and it is very possible that the Reverend John Norton, the minister in Timothy and Mary's church, did as well.[215] The Congregational church in Chatham was a primitive building, simply furnished with repeating square box pews where families would sit and listen to Norton preach from a white pulpit. As the political tensions increased and Norton's sermons echoed his congregation's concerns, it is possible that even usually restless children, who sometimes turned the loose balusters surrounding the pews, causing entertaining squeaks, actually listened intently to the calls toward freedom.[216]

When the British Parliament enacted further restrictive measures on Massachusetts in 1774, surrounding colonies responded in kind with additional acts of protest. The Connecticut Assembly adopted resolutions denouncing Parliamentary actions. And in numerous town meetings across New England, the people voted to help the inhabitants of Boston, allotting them food and money. In East Haddam itself, just such a resolution was passed on June 30. At that same venue, representatives from the town also resolved to establish a committee designed expressly to relay the town's support to Boston and to ensure that the residents of their own town were well-informed as to the events of the developing crisis.[217] Committees like this were created throughout much of New England. Support for the struggle against England was especially strong along the Connecticut River Valley. In a particularly militant act, on September 14 residents hoisted a huge flag, portraying the liberty of America against the tyranny of England, on a flagpole 147 feet high at East Haddam landing, and thus in the direct purview of all those traveling along the Connecticut River. The event was celebrated by many in the town with cheers and the firing of muskets.[218]

The town of Chatham, where Timothy and Mary lived, also vowed support for the cause of liberty. A special vigilance committee of eleven prominent members of the community was established to oversee a boycott of British-made goods.[219] Although these boycotts were enacted in many communities it is particularly significant that the inhabitants of Chatham supported them, as so many residents there made their living in the sea trade or in shipbuilding, thereby endorsing a measure for the greater good that directly negatively affected their individual livelihoods.

For years following the end of the French and Indian War, the required militia training days held a few times a year throughout New England had become social affairs. Mary would gather with neighbors and family while Timothy and the men from Chatham performed military drills in a disinterested fashion. With the conquest of French Canada and the defeat of many of the Indians on the frontier, the need for military exactness was far less pressing. But this feeling changed as tension with Parliament mounted. Men in Chatham, and all over New England, began to take the drills seriously again and to practice more frequently. Timothy, a lieutenant in the local militia, like other officers from the preceding war used his experience to train the men in earnest. With Captain Silas Dunham, Timothy organized their Chatham militia to be able to respond quickly if called.

Messengers were sent on April 19, 1775, from Lexington and Concord in Massachusetts. The news of the deadly skirmish with British soldiers reached the community of Chatham within a few days. Signal guns boomed along the Connecticut River, disrupting the busy spring schedule of farmers throughout the river valley.[220] Responding immediately, Captain Dunham and Timothy worked feverishly, assembling thirty-six[221] men to march to the aid of Massachusetts. Reverend Norton had served in the two previous wars, but his age prevented his joining this time. His son served instead, and the reverend surely blessed them all and encouraged them to endure their future trials, for their cause was righteous. Timothy and the others hastened to Boston, meeting many of the thousands of Connecticut men marching along the winding roads on the same mission. Timothy's younger brother, Sergeant Gordon Percival, may have met Timothy on those crowded roads as he marched with the militia from East Haddam.[222] There had been no official call from the Connecticut Assembly to muster. This mass migration of armed men represented a spontaneous answer to a call for help from a fellow colony—a shared sense of duty to defend their beliefs and liberties.

The British troops withdrew back to Boston after the fight on April 19. Now that the immediate threat had ended, many of the colonial militia units headed home. In their haste the volunteers had not made arrangements for a long-term commitment to service. Timothy and the men from Chatham served for five days before returning to Chatham.[223]

In response to the crisis at Boston, the Connecticut Assembly called for a special session to meet on April 26. The session lasted until May 6 and called for the mobilization of one fourth of the Connecticut militia to be formed into six regiments. This force would face the British army for a longer duration. Five of the men in Timothy's Chatham alarm company signed up to serve in the second company of the Second Regiment under the command of Joseph Spencer. A few of Mary's relatives and many others they knew from East Haddam formed the first company in this regiment.[224] At this time, Timothy decided to stay home. While Spencer's regiment headed toward Boston, Timothy and Mary busily finished the spring planting and made arrangements to prepare for Timothy's eventual service in defense of New England. During this hectic period, some of their neighbors fought at the Battle of Bunker Hill on June 17.[225] This bloody battle dimmed the prospect of a peaceful settlement between the American colonies and Britain and hardened the feelings of antagonism on both sides. Even though the American forces lost the battle and suffered around five hundred casualties, the British figure was nearly double that. This helped regenerate American confidence since the British army was thought to have some of the finest soldiers in the world.

Timothy's chance to serve came soon after Bunker Hill when the Connecticut Assembly authorized the formation of two more regiments in July. He was commissioned as first lieutenant in the ninth company of the Eighth Connecticut Regiment. Colonel Jedidiah Huntington, from Norwich, would command the regiment. Timothy started his service on July 6. Most of the officers in his company were from Haddam, Connecticut; therefore, many of the soldiers were familiar to him. And six of them from Chatham had raced with him toward Boston back in April.[226] The fact that Timothy had time to prepare for his departure from home certainly did not make leaving Mary and his children any easier. It had now been almost fifteen years since his last military campaign.

Timothy's company was the first in the regiment to finish assembling; all seventy men signed up together on July 9. For most of the month they served with the Seventh Connecticut Regiment, guarding the coast along Long Island Sound. In August, Colonel Huntington and seven of his companies were ordered to join the Continental Army around Boston, now under the command of General George Washington, from Virginia. Timothy's company and two others, as well as the Seventh Connecticut Regiment, remained to guard the Connecticut and Rhode Island coastline from British naval vessels on plundering expeditions. General Washington ordered the Seventh Connecticut and the rest of the Eighth Connecticut to march to Boston after he received information that the British there were expecting reinforcements of fifteen thousand men. Mercifully, the report proved to be inflated, but Washington concentrated his army around Boston regardless during the last two weeks of September.[227]

By the time Timothy arrived in Roxbury, Massachusetts, on September 30, the nights were already getting cold.[228] The preceding evening had brought the first frost to the Boston area.[229] The men in Timothy's company had to find space in the crowded camp, and raise their tents in lines marked off as company streets. They were assigned cooking areas and shown where the necessaries (or latrines) and garbage pits were located. Since the rest of the regiment had been in this camp for over seven weeks, all the best locations had been long before claimed, and supplies of straw for bedding in the tents would have been scarce.

Over the next few days, Timothy and his men were briefed on the news and activities of the rest of the regiment since their separation in August. There had not been enough tents when they first arrived. Being exposed to the weather, many men had become sick and some had already died. Very few had been injured from the near-daily British bombardment upon their positions, though one man from the regiment had been gruesomely mangled and killed when a large twelve-pound cannonball lodged in his body.[230] Supplies were lacking for the army, with the shortage of powder especially critical. As early as August, officers in the regiment had been asked to contribute personal funds to purchase powder.[231] For Timothy, it must have felt just like his first chaotic campaign in 1755 all over again. As in the past, the men suffered while waiting for the army to create a properly supplied organization.

When Timothy arrived, the siege of Boston was in a stalemate. The British now controlled Boston and the Charlestown peninsula, which included Bunker Hill. The American army surrounded Boston from Dorchester in the south through Roxbury and Cambridge to the hills northwest of Boston. Both sides had constructed strong fortifications protecting their positions. Since the Battle of Bunker Hill, neither army had initiated a direct move against the other, only miscellaneous raiding jabs.

Timothy's camp at the town of Roxbury was opposite the one piece of land connecting Boston to the mainland, a thin stretch appropriately named Boston Neck. Timothy's regiment joined the Second Connecticut, the Sixth Connecticut, and three Massachusetts regiments, all under the command of Brigadier General Joseph Spencer, the very man who had led Timothy's company in his last two campaigns in the previous war. Spencer's brigade had the job of guarding this important access to Boston, and the men labored arduously to build protective earthworks facing the British. Timothy had much experience commanding men at this type of work, having performed the likes of it at Fort William Henry, Fort Edward, Fort Ontario, and Fort Stanwix. Clearly the work was vital, as attested on October 6 when the British launched a large cannonade upon the American positions around Roxbury. The earthworks held, however, and only one man was wounded and two cows killed.[232]

Roxbury extended nearly eight miles east to west, and about two miles north to south. It contained over two hundred dwellings, one hundred sixty barns, and some mills and other businesses. The town had been a beautiful place; forests, hills, and a large pond occupied the spaces between the gambrel-roofed homes and a number of mansions. By the time Timothy arrived, the town had already been transformed. Eight miles of earthwork fortifications had been dug through the town, and the prominent hills were now studded with earthen forts complete with walls twelve feet thick and five feet high. Most of the population had been evacuated, and many buildings deemed to provide cover for an advancing enemy had been torn down. Many of the remaining structures had already been smashed by enemy cannonballs or burned by exploding shells. Valuable orchard trees had been cut down, their branches sharpened, and made into fields of obstacles on the desolate eight hundred yards of ground between the opposing American and British fortifications. Windows had been removed or shot through, and broken-brick and plaster dust covered the interiors of once-pleasant homes. The once-bountiful fields were unattended, and many of the crops had been destroyed. A Congregational meetinghouse in town, which sat on a hill, had become a favorite target of the British artillery. Its punctured yet still-erect steeple stood in symbolic defiance of the British, but its use as a place of worship was terminated for the duration of the siege. Until this point, Timothy had fought all his campaigns along the wilderness frontier. This was the first time he had to face the destructive power of artillery on New England farms and towns—places so close to his heart.[233]

The town of Roxbury had become a temporary home for thousands of American soldiers. The men needed wood for cooking fires and maintaining their general warmth, and the fences throughout town became a convenient source. Many of the vacant homes and barns were used to quarter officers and soldiers during the siege. Two large homes near the seventy-acre Jamaica pond were abandoned by Tory owners who had chosen to remain loyal to the British King. These were converted into military hospitals. One of these had been the home of Commodore Joshua Loring, who had commanded the small English flotilla of ships on Lake Ontario and the Saint Lawrence River during Timothy's last campaign in 1760. Loring's old backyard became a graveyard for men who succumbed to disease.[234]

The daily routine of life in a military camp was tedious. Drums would wake the soldiers and sound again when they were to sleep. They would line up in formation in the morning; report those too ill for duty; listen to the daily orders; and learn the parole or password for the day, which they would need in order to pass through the many guard stations around camp and the earthworks facing the British lines. If they were assigned to work on defensive positions that day, the officers were required to make note of exactly what axes, spades, and other tools were issued so that those tools could be accounted for when the work was done. Muskets were inspected regularly, and those found amiss were to be cleaned or turned in to the regimental armorer for repair. Any time soldiers were to be punished for disciplinary problems, the regiment would assemble in formation to witness the striking of lashes upon the condemned's back. As of October 12, Timothy's regiment held drills at two each afternoon for all those not occupied with other duties.[235] Throughout the day and night, men were posted on guard duty and officers were assigned to oversee the guards. So that the guards would not be distracted from noticing a possible enemy approach, the noise in camp had to be policed and limited as well. Those soldiers unfamiliar with the restrictive nature of military life grumbled and counted the days until their service was scheduled to end. For most of the Connecticut troops that day had been charted to be December 10.[236]

General Washington faced one of the many crises of his military career during the fall of 1775. Since the men in his army had enlisted for a limited period, he needed to reenlist a new army under the very noses of the enemy without them discovering how weakened the American forces would be during the transition. He initially tried to solve the problem by asking men from the different colonies to extend their enlistments. For the officers from Connecticut, Washington requested they stay only a few weeks longer than their scheduled date, now until January 1, 1776. And he asked the officers to request that their men to do the same.[237]

After a series of dark and gloomy days, Timothy met with all the officers in the regiment on October 21 to discuss the issue of staying on past December 10, and whether the men would stay as well. The cold rain that fell during this meeting added to the muddy, uncomfortable conditions in camp. The officers decided to ask the men during the next morning's formation,[238] surely hoping that the rain would stop before they had to put forth such an important question. Indeed the next day dawned without rain, but the morning formation was a sour occasion anyway. The men reacted vehemently in opposition to serving beyond their proscribed terms. Even a special sermon given later that day by Reverend William Gordon, recently returned from his duty as chaplin of the Continental Congress in Philadelphia, failed to sway them.[239]

On the twenty-fourth, formal orders arrived requesting all the officers to make known their intent regarding another year's service. Discussions continued and the situation grew uglier with numbers of men gathering and yelling mutinous slogans that evening. Order was restored, but tension persisted. October 25 brought a very cold dawn as the officers continued their discussions of extended service and methods to control threatening outbreaks of mutiny. Warmer weather the next day may have eased the situation slightly and reduced the seditious rumblings in the ranks, but the ever-looming problems of maintaining an army and standing up against the British for their rights, of course, endured.[240] Timothy would continue to serve, but close to a third of the current officers would not. The dreary siege of Boston continued. The only comforting news Timothy could have shared with his men were the frequent rumors of deserting British soldiers describing food shortages in Boston and the miserable conditions they had experienced while under siege. Considering the suffering of the men in the American army and the shortages of crucial supplies on that side, too, it seemed to require a miracle to raise a new army in the middle of winter while still besieging the British in Boston. To Timothy, as to others, the motto on one side of their orange regimental flag, "An Appeal to Heaven," must have seemed particularly apropos at that juncture.[241]

If Timothy's duties allowed, he may have attended the funeral of a fellow officer from Spencer's Second Connecticut Regiment on October 30. Considering his relationship with Spencer, he most likely joined the service. This would have given him a chance to visit with old neighbors from East Haddam who served in the first company of the Second Connecticut and to swap stories of home with the Chatham men who served in the second company. The funeral was for Amos Wadsworth, who had died the day before. The viewing of the deceased was held in a large house appropriated from another Tory family who had probably fled to the shelter of the British in Boston. The coffin was then placed on a bier, or movable platform, in the yard, and covered with a black velvet and silk cloth with six tassels. Two swords lay crossed on the coffin. Leading the military procession were twenty soldiers in formation, followed by sergeants of the regiment acting as bearers. Following the coffin were the grieving family members riding in three carriages surrounded by the officers of Spencer's regiment, and other officers from the army. Next in the procession marched the entire Second Regiment behind its blue standard with a black ribbon attached to the top of the staff. The drummers and fifers played a funeral march for the distance of a mile and a half along the road to Brookline. For the last half mile of the event, the church bell in Brookline chimed incessantly. It was both a solemn and magnificent ceremony.[242]

The next eight days were mostly wet and cold, and largely uneventful. The monotony was briefly broken on November 9 when the British landed troops on Lechmere Point, across the Back Bay from Boston, and skirmished with the American forces stationed there. Beating drums called the men in Timothy's regiment into quick assemblage. His company's muskets and ammunition were inspected in preparation for battle, but it did not march because the British withdrew from the attack before Timothy's regiment was needed. Instead, the men passed another stormy night in camp. On Sunday, November 12, the cold wind was so strong that the regularly scheduled sermon was cancelled. That night the British advanced a small force against the American lines at Roxbury. The guards on duty effectively drove the British back with musket fire, quelling the danger quickly, but not before the camp awoke to the sounds of the attack. It was another cold night, making it all the more difficult for the men to fall back to sleep.[243]

The officers of the Eighth Connecticut Regiment who were planning to reenlist were called to a meeting with Colonel Huntington on November 14. They discussed the organization of their new 1776 regiment and the challenging process of trying to recruit men to fill it.[244] Theirs was to be renamed the Seventeenth Continental Regiment. The term "continental" implied that their army was a united American force, no longer a conglomerate of varied regiments raised from different colonies. The new regiment would have only eight companies instead of the present ten, and Timothy was promoted to captain. Over half of the Eighth Connecticut's officers would serve again sometime in the forthcoming year, but only seventeen, fewer than half, would be in the new Seventeenth Regiment. New officers were needed across the board, and eleven deserving men were promoted from the ranks to fill the open slots. Timothy must have been proud that two officers and a sergeant were promoted from his company but also disheartened to part with them when they were all reassigned to other companies. Timothy was given three new officers, all of whom had served in 1775, albeit in different companies. He would soon get to know them well when they commenced working together to reenlist men.[245]

The fact that officers in the new companies were from different towns and not well known to one another, not to mention to the men, made recruiting even more difficult. The men were accustomed to serving under officers from their own community; further, they were keenly familiar with their officer's mannerisms and abilities, and were not pleased that this custom had changed. Moreover, in the past, soldiers enlisted for campaigns that usually did not span the winter months. Now Timothy and the other officers were recruiting for service in the dead of winter. Considering these abundant obstacles, a decision was made to discharge many of the officers before the men so that they could begin recruiting as soon as possible. Colonel Huntington hoped that after the men had a chance to recuperate at home, they might become more interested in reenlisting.[246]

The rest of November was ridden with poor weather—cold rain, storms, snow, and strong blustery winds. Fortunately, the men were well supplied with food and able to enjoy two feasts. They celebrated the traditional Connecticut Thanksgiving on November 16 and Massachusetts's on the twenty-third. But the later festivities were cut short when they were ordered to prepare for a suspected British attack that evening which ultimately did not materialize.[247]

Colonel Huntington was actually absent part of this time, attending his ill wife, Faith Huntington, who was staying in the nearby town of Dedham. Her physical health did improve, but her despondency about the war was reportedly so grave that it may have driven her to commit suicide. She hanged herself on November 24. Faith was the daughter of the Connecticut governor, Jonathan Trumbull, so Timothy may have attended another large funeral on November 28. Another stormy, wet night followed, further augmenting the already gloomy morale in camp.[248]

The camps had become quagmires of cold mud. In some areas, shoes could be sucked right off the soldiers' feet as they slipped their way between tents or trudged to their morning formations. Many had tried to ameliorate the situation by adding boards of wood, brick, stone, even turf around their tents. In addition, a few shacks had been constructed, complete with windows and doors. By all reports, the soldiers existed more like wretched refugees than the ranks of a properly supplied military army.[249]

Rebellion erupted on December 1 when some of the Connecticut soldiers simply marched off without orders.[250] The tension in camp was obviously compounded by the strain on the men's morale by the death of two members of Timothy's company during December.[251] The lack of proper sanitary conditions in the camps, and a dearth of warm clothing for the cold season, contributed to many deaths from dysentery, typhus, and typhoid fever. Timothy knew from firsthand experience that sanitary control was critical, but other less experienced officers and many of the men did not understand its importance. Not only were the open latrines a concern, but so were the ill-disciplined men who often chose to relieve themselves along the edge of camp, filling the place with vile odor and contaminating the water supply.[252] On top of all this, fear spread that smallpox might soon enter the American army because it had broken out in Boston.[253]

General Washington was furious over the Connecticut troops' stubborn refusal to stay past December 10. Many of the other New England troops who remained rebuked the Connecticut men as well. Still nothing could change their minds. The ramshackle conditions of the camps and the plague of lice-infested clothing on the men discouraged the lot of them. As expected, on Sunday, the tenth, the men collected their pay and left.[254] It wasn't until they returned to Connecticut and faced the reproach of kin and neighbors that many decided to reenlist. Meanwhile, General Washington had to order other militia units to serve around Boston as replacements. Fortunately, the British did not attack the American besiegers during this vulnerable period.

Timothy made the trip home and enjoyed part of December with his family. While there, he caught up on local news and events and learned of the trials Mary and his children had faced running the farm while he had been away. Mercifully, Timothy's brother, Rowland, was nearby to help Mary. Timothy likely tried to work on neglected projects at home as much as he could, but the heavy responsibility of recruiting soldiers for his new company probably occupied the majority of his time.

Timothy returned to his regiment at Roxbury in January. The search for volunteers had been difficult. He had even recruited his son, also named Timothy, as a private.[255] It was certainly tough for Mary to watch both her husband and son leave, but she was steadfast in her support for the struggle and had come to realize, like so many left behind, that every possible man was needed to overcome the British forces. Timothy's reassembled regiment finally contained around four hundred men, still far short of the stipulated goal of 688.[256] Most of the other regiments fell just as short of manpower; moreover, the whole army was severely lacking a plethora of supplies ranging from tents, blankets, arms, and powder, to money. The weather hardly mitigated the situation as snow covered the landscape and the freezing temperatures made life in camp miserable.

General Spencer's brigade was reorganized at this time to include Colonel Parson's Tenth Regiment, Colonel Huntington's Seventeenth, Colonel Webb's Nineteenth, and Colonel Wylly's Twenty-second.[257] Consequently, the new brigade now included only Connecticut regiments. Timothy must have been pleased to be so proximate to the Twenty-second Regiment, as many of its members were from East Haddam and Chatham. Marcus Cole, who had been a sergeant in the Chatham alarm company back in April of the preceding year with Timothy, had now been promoted to a lieutenant in the Twenty-second. Overall, however, far fewer of Timothy's friends and neighbors were still serving the cause. Many had ultimately not reenlisted, and others, like Lieutenant Samuel Cooper of Chatham, had perished. Cooper had bravely joined the grueling expedition led by General Benedict Arnold against British-controlled Canada and had been killed during the failed assault of Quebec City on December 31.[258]

By the end of January, more recruits had fortunately joined the army, but most regiments remained far below their quotas, and now there was little hope of attracting more. Timothy's regiment was not only short of men, but also did not have enough muskets for those who had enlisted. Colonel Huntington reported on February 8 that he still needed about ninety muskets—a pretty grave problem indeed.[259] The shortage of arms prevailed throughout the entire American army. In response, many long spears had been distributed to the troops to help better defend their lines, but they were a shoddy replacement when weighed against the effects of musket fire.[260] The frozen ground retarded the work of constructing earthen fortifications around Boston and further delayed plans of action overall. Meanwhile, the men collected sticks and bundled them together to form fascines, and wove others together to form gabions, for use in the future as siding for new earthen walls.

The harsh winter weather and deep snow brought much suffering to the ill-equipped soldiers around Boston. Still, there was one benefit of the winter snows: they allowed Colonel Knox to retrieve artillery from Fort Ticonderoga in New York. Knox used giant sleds to drag the fifty-eight guns and mortars collected from the wilderness fort over the snow-covered mountains of western Massachusetts back to Washington's troops surrounding Boston. It was a torturous journey of three hundred miles, pulling close to sixty tons of valuable siege artillery. The hope was that these large guns, if properly placed, could break the stalemate of the siege.

The right placement for the new guns was deemed to be Dorchester Heights, a rocky peninsula east of Roxbury. Two hills, both twice as high as Bunker Hill and with steeper ascents, formed this site that was within artillery range of both Boston and much of the harbor. Curiously, the British had not occupied this key position. Considering the British were willing to expend so many lives to gain control of the Charlestown peninsula (which included Bunker and Breed's hills) on June 17, 1775, it was especially peculiar that they did nothing to gain the more valuable Dorchester Heights. General Washington was not going to make the same mistake, and he spent much of February planning to fortify the site and position his new artillery there.

The preparations were extensive, for the operation faced a number of serious logistical hurdles. First, just getting the men, materials, and heavy guns there meant crossing a low open stretch of land that sometimes flooded during high tide and could be easily fired upon by British artillery in Boston. Additionally, they faced the now common challenge that the ground on the heights would be too frozen to dig earthworks for a proper defense. Finally, the position had to be made somehow defendable in one night to prevent the British from attacking before the Americans were ready. Lacking any sort of professional military engineers like those in the British forces, it was left to pure American ingenuity to tackle these pressing, multiple problems.

For Dorchester Heights to be occupied in one night everything had to be carefully planned and constructed. Hay bundles were collected to form an artillery-proof wall that would be laid to cover the low causeway leading to the heights.[261] Timber frames were constructed that, once placed on the heights, would be filled with hay bales, bundles of branches called fascines, and wooden barrels filled with dirt to form an adequate protective wall.[262] Details of soldiers searched the towns around Boston for the three hundred wagons, carts, and oxen needed to move the loads of equipment. In the hospitals, extra bandages were made and more beds acquired in anticipation of heavy casualties.[263] Colonel Huntington even requested an extra doctor from his home in Connecticut to come help bolster the thin medical corps.[264] Timothy's regiment in Roxbury bustled with activity not seen for months. The men certainly felt a new purpose that cast away the sorry malaise that had gripped them for too long.

General Spencer's Connecticut brigade and a Massachusetts brigade, together about three thousand men, would execute the tricky move to Dorchester Heights. If the British attacked them in force, General Putnam would be ready in Cambridge with about four thousand additional men primed to cross the Back Bay by boat and attack Boston.[265] If by turn the British did nothing, the artillery on Dorchester Heights would control the harbor, thereby forcing the British to leave Boston or starve. And if the British retaliated by attacking the Americans on the heights, they might well leave Boston too weak to fend off General Putnam's advance. Washington focused on victory whichever way the enemy responded. Considering the British had about nine thousand soldiers as well as additional sailors and marines[266] in Boston, compared to the Americans' total of roughly ten thousand, the plan was still a gamble.[267] Even activating two thousand Massachusetts militiamen[268] for the operation did not augment Washington's strength with respect to the well-drilled professional British soldiers.

The night of March 4 was selected for the operation, based in part on the schedule of the tides and progress of the preparations. Beginning on March 2, Washington ordered a nightly bombardment of the British positions in an effort to both distract them and muffle the construction noises emanating from the American camps.[269] Timothy's men became nocturnal, working vigorously under the rumbling cannon fire and the burning fuses of shells arching across the dark sky toward the British lines.

By the designated evening of March 4, Timothy and his men were finally prepared, albeit anxious. The nightly cannonade recommenced; this time the intensity of the fire from both sides was greater than the previous two nights.[270] The full moon became framed by streaks of fire from the glowing fuses on the numerous artillery shells overhead. Timothy could have heard the cries of women in Boston seeking shelter as his regiment hastened its advance.[271]

Leading the advancing procession were riflemen from the frontier regions of the west.[272] They typically wore hunting shirts, buckskin breeches, leggings, and moccasins. They were armed with long-barreled rifles, native to Pennsylvania but rarely seen in New England.[273] Along with their rifles they carried tomahawks and long knives in the Indian-style belts around their waists. These characters could easily have reminded Timothy of the Rangers he worked with in the last war. Both displayed a serious lack of discipline while in the camps, and a maddening disregard for authority. Still, the riflemen's acute skill at long-range shooting was an invaluable asset to the American army and was greatly feared by British officers—the riflemen's favorite targets. Thus this vital American advance would be well screened and guarded by the rakish frontiersmen.

Fortunately for them, ground fog protected the Americans from view in that critical low area between Roxbury and Dorchester Heights.[274] Timothy and his men marched along beside creaking wagons, heavily laden with equipment, through the mist that perfectly screened them from British sentries only a half mile away on Boston Neck. The entire column was very tense and quiet as it moved past the bundles of hay laid out to protect the men's crossing to the heights.[275] Up out of the fog, Timothy and his men finally ascended Dorchester Heights under the bright moon. The weather was uncommonly warm for early March and made for a perfect night for hard labor. Timothy led his men to their assigned duties on what was soon looking very much like a rocky anthill of intense activity. Soldiers assembled the wooden frames, then filled them with the prefabricated fascines, gabions, barrels, and bales of hay. The wagons traveled back and forth delivering the supplies like clockwork. Many carts made three or four trips. The rise in temperature even thawed the ground enough to allow men to break up the earth with picks, while others quickly shoveled the dirt over the frames filled with hay. All the while, the incessant, heavy bombardment muted the sounds of construction. Within only a few hours, two large forts and a number of smaller works had been nearly completed; and by three o'clock in the morning the troops from Roxbury were in position guarding the new line while continuing to enhance its defensibility as best they could.[276] The British switched their fire to the Heights at dawn, finally realizing what the Americans were doing.[277] Timothy was relieved at three o'clock by a fresh force moving into the site. He guided his men off as the British cannon fire intensified. Fortunately, most of the cannonballs fell short and did no harm. Timothy's men staggered back to Roxbury exhausted, but undoubtedly proud of their hard, fine work.[278]

The early morning light revealed to the astonished British the full extent of the new American fortifications. They found it unbelievable that such a strong position had been constructed overnight.[279] As the British stood in awe and grappled with a plan of response, Timothy had his men rest to recharge their energies so they could better resist the expected enemy attack. It had been a long night of toil, but well worthwhile. Now the American army firmly held the strategic heights, well equipped with artillery in strong fortifications. The British were forced to make a move.

General Howe, in command of the British at Boston, assembled his officers by mid-morning and, after consulting with them, committed to an attack of the heights as soon as possible. Two thousand soldiers and enough boats for them were gathered for the assault that night. The whole harbor bustled with activity.[280]

Washington observed the enemy movements as he inspected the defenses on Dorchester Heights. He made several observations and suggested some improvements, but overall he was pleased with the successful night's operation.[281] He then prepared his men to repel the difficult assault he actually wanted the British to make. Washington knew that if they approached, the steeper hills would pose a greater problem than those the British had encountered at the battle of Bunker Hill. And this time the Americans had more artillery.[282] Washington hoped the enemy soldiers would smash themselves against the Heights, and consequently have a higher casualty rate than on that horrid June day the year prior.

General Howe continued his preparations throughout the day of March 5, but bad weather intervened that night.[283] By sunset, snow, sleet, and hail were falling upon both armies. The wind achieved hurricane strength and ripped through the area. Those Americans in tents struggled to keep their canvas shelters from blowing away, consequently expending much of the night hammering tent pegs back into the ground. Those men billeted in buildings were much more comfortable but not entirely safe from the wrath of the storm; some blasts of wind were strong enough to smash in windows, scattering shards of glass into the rooms.[284] Due to the wild weather, the expected British attack was postponed and finally canceled.

Over the next couple of weeks both sides exchanged artillery shells, but the siege was clearly approaching termination. The British decided to withdraw and left Boston on March 17.[285] While the British did not depart the harbor area until after March 27,[286] the siege had been won, and the American army entered the city of Boston as the clear victors.

Timothy celebrated their victory with the men of the Seventeenth Continental Regiment. Their devoted, grueling efforts had resulted in the expulsion of the powerful British Army from Boston—no small feat to be sure. Hopes were raised. This triumph magnified ambitions for independence from Britain. Early that year, the army had become likewise emboldened when copies of Thomas Paine's newly published *Common Sense* had been distributed. This widely read document urged a declaration of independence from England and was greatly responsible for changing the nature of the conflict from simply fighting for the rights of Englishmen to the now-overarching goal of the creation of a new nation. Timothy must have looked to the future as far brighter in prospects. All told, the spring weather of 1776 represented far more than an end of a dreadful winter; it seemed to forebode a bright new beginning for them all.

CHAPTER 6

Longest Campaign

After the British withdrawal from Boston, the people of the thirteen American colonies breathed a collective sigh of relief. Some even assumed that they had won the armed conflict. General Washington knew better and began to make plans to counter the enemy's next move. He determined that New York City, given its valuable harbor, would be the target of the next British campaign; accordingly, he began moving his army there from Boston.

Timothy's regiment left Roxbury on April 4.[287] After being stuck in the frigid camps during the siege of Boston, it was a pleasant change to be moving again. The men's morale improved and the spring weather fueled hopes of positive change. Along the roads people would cheer the men and provide food and further encouragement. In fact, the long relocation to New York actually resembled, in part, a victory parade. The people were proud of their army and their victory at Boston.[288] Timothy could very well have found it more challenging to maintain the discipline in his company under such festive auspices. Two of Timothy's men, Corporal John Strong and Benjamin Tubbs, actually deserted the company during this period, forcing him to place a notice in the April 22 edition of the *Connecticut Courant* offering a reward for the return of either or both of them.[289] Overall, officers like Timothy were faced with the challenge of keeping their men focused on the future struggle while many around them were acting under the false assumption that the war was already won.

Colonel Huntington found it difficult to find enough transportation with which to relocate the regiment's equipment; therefore it took more than a month to fully reassemble in New York.[290] By April 26, only six companies of the regiment had arrived there, and they set up camp just outside the city.[291]

At the time, New York City had a population of around twenty-five thousand. Although larger, it was nonetheless much like Boston in that the city was highly concentrated in a small area near the harbor on the southern end of what was named York Island. Bordering the island on the west was the wide Hudson River, also known as the North River. On the opposite side there was the East River, complete with a section of treacherous crosscurrents aptly named Hell's Gate, which separated the island from the mainland and the much larger Long Island farther to the east. The city's brick housing was much like that of Boston, but some of the streets were wider, such as the tree-lined Broadway, which was the area's principal throughway, replete with public buildings, churches, and many more homes. At the southern end of Broadway lay Fort George, a square bastion eighty feet long on each side. The stone outer walls had been constructed along the shoreline during the last war, and they remained the only fortifications created to protect the entire harbor. Broadway continued north from Fort George, past Trinity Church through an open market area named Oswego, past Saint Paul's Chapel and the open field of the Common and, after another mile, moved out of the city near a freshwater pond.[292]

The harbor's docks were, for the most part, on the southeast side of the city, facing the East River. Queen Street, a couple of blocks in from the docks, was the principal business thoroughfare. Bowery Lane was the main road leaving the city; it split off Broadway at the Commons, heading northeast, and then north to the Outward. The Outward encompassed the rest of York Island and was sparsely populated with farms and large estates built around streams, marshes, and woods. On the far northern end of the island, rocky ground mixed with woods. The one connection with the mainland was King's Bridge, a wooden structure spanning from the northern tip of the island.[293]

It was obvious that the British, known for their strong navy, could easily navigate the numerous waterways around the city to their advantage, so the Americans worked to erect fortifications intended to counter them. While the American army did not have the battlefield experience of the British army, they did know how to dig. Fortifications sprang up all along the shoreline of New York harbor during that spring of 1776. On the Long Island side of the harbor, Fort Defiance now guarded the Red Hook peninsula and Fort Stirling the ferry between Brooklyn and New York City. Governors Island became one of the most strongly fortified areas in the harbor. On the northwest end of Manhattan Island, Fort Washington was constructed on the rocky Harlem Heights overlooking the Hudson River. Opposite Fort Washington on the New Jersey side was Fort Lee. Still another fortification overlooked Hell's Gate on the east side of the island. All told, the city of New York was soon encircled by forts and earthworks. Even the open streets facing the water's edge were barricaded.[294]

Timothy's regiment with the rest of General Spencer's brigade camped northeast of the city near the Rutgers farm at Corlear's Hook.[295] This was a beautiful piece of high ground, overlooking the city to one side and the East River to the other. Timothy would have seen the sun rise over Long Island and, after a long day of overseeing his men dig, its setting over the New Jersey hills to the west. Military drills were infrequent.

Though they desperately needed the practice, the construction projects were considered a priority. The men labored with picks, shovels, and whatever other tools they could find. As spring advanced to summer, their clothes began to wear out and were in constant need of repair. On the days it did not rain, dust would choke their lungs and cling to their sweat. Rain showers held the dust back, but lengthy downpours turned the construction sites into mud pits. Either way, meager soap rations were probably depleted much too quickly.[296]

By June, Timothy's men could really feel their progress as the fortifications began to finally take form. Fort Spencer was a star-shaped bastion anchoring the southern end of their defenses. It stood on a rise overlooking the shipyards of the city and would hold two twelve-pound artillery pieces and four smaller guns. From Fort Spencer a line of entrenchments arched northward, following the contour of the hill to a circular redoubt named Jones's Hill. There, emplacements for eight artillery pieces were constructed. The trench line continued westward until it reached Bowery Lane. This defense line faced north and protected the city from an overland attack from that direction. In keeping with this mission, two smaller circular redoubts, both able to hold artillery, were placed along the trench. One, the Bayard's Hill Redoubt, was on the west side of Bowery Lane, on a prominent hill. The walls of this daunting fortification assumed an irregular shape, combining the pattern of a star and a diamond. The eight nine-pound guns, four three-pound guns, and six mortars that were mounted at Bayard's Hill could fire over the harbor docks to the south or on any force approaching from the north along Bowery Lane. Still other redoubts and earthworks extended further west, and many smaller defensive positions were scattered around. Thus, just as they had done around Boston the year before, the Americans transformed New York City into an amazing collection of defensive positions.[297]

June 4 came and went without the usual festive celebrations of the King of England's birthday. Many colonists around and in New York City were actually still loyal to the King of

England, but they kept a low profile for fear of persecution by the rebels now in control of the city. One example of such abuse occurred on Monday night, the tenth of June, when a number of Tories were forced through the streets of the city holding candles. The angry crowds pushed the candles into the faces of the loyalists, burning their skin with the flames and hot wax.[298] Two days later, the situation worsened when more Tories were carried through the streets in broad daylight and were verbally and physically tortured. They were made to straddle a rail, stripped of much of their clothing, and paraded through the taunting crowds. The affair escalated into a riot that was extremely difficult for the Continental soldiers to quell.[299]

The potential for conflict between Tories and rebels only increased when, later in the month, a plot to aid the British was uncovered. Tories, it was discovered, were planning to enlist American soldiers to actually come to the aid of the British during the attack on New York City. Furthermore, rumors of plots to assassinate American generals, including Washington, swept through the soldiers' camps adding to the already tense atmosphere there. Many of the conspirators were hauled into prison, and one guilty soldier, from General Washington's personal guard, was condemned to death. The gallows for his execution was constructed beside Timothy's regimental camp in a field next to Bowery Lane. Thousands of soldiers and local residents witnessed the actual event on the morning of June 28.[300] A guard of eighty soldiers marched the condemned, William Hickey, to the gallows. Hickey did not exhibit any signs of remorse, though he burst into tears as the chaplain said his final words. Shortly after eleven in the morning Hickey expired, his lifeless limbs left dangling from the rope.[301] Still, this hardly mitigated fears of further Tory interference, which were soon realized later in July when another plot was unveiled, this one involving plans to destroy two large frigates under construction further up the Hudson River.[302] Contrary to the situation in Boston, a large percentage of the population of New York City remained loyal to the King, prompting officers like Timothy to keep his camp sentries ever vigilant.

Several British ships had been lingering outside New York harbor for most of the year, but on June 29 an enormous fleet of 130 ships arrived.[303] Following this threat, on July 1 the men in Timothy's company were made to wake early so that they could fix their meal and be on duty by six o'clock. At nine o'clock, the alarm cannon fired again. With that, Timothy had to collect his company, have the men's weapons and equipment inspected, and hurry them along to their designated station.[304] It turned out that the British had landed a small force on Long Island with the intention of testing the American defenses, and General Washington felt he had to reinforce his troops there in case it turned into a major attack. Washington ordered General Spencer to supply the extra soldiers, so Timothy's camp burst into action as five hundred men were quickly organized and marched to the ferry. By the time Spencer's men made the crossing to Brooklyn, the British had withdrawn to their ships.[305] Nonetheless, the nerve-racking routine of responding to alarms became part of Timothy's company's regular activities as day after day more British ships arrived and anchored south of the city, in full view of the American army.

News of the thirteen colonies' declaration of independence from England reached the soldiers within the first week of July.[306] On July 9, Timothy's regiment assembled in parade formation at six in the evening when the entire Declaration of Independence was read to them.[307] Public readings took place in all the camps, alerting the troops to the important news that the war had entered a new phase.[308] They were now engaged in a more daunting struggle—a revolution to create a brand new nation. Cheers resounded at the news in all the camps in and around New York. Local supporters of the rebellion gathered in the streets and swarmed down Broadway to the giant statue of King George the Third on horseback, where they eagerly proceeded to pull the statue down with rope and tools they had gathered along the way. People hacked off parts in a frenzied jubilation and placed the monarch's severed head on display on a pole in front of a local tavern.[309] Eventually, most of the statue's lead parts would be hauled into Connecticut to be melted down and turned into rebel musket balls.[310]

Timothy's daily tasks were interrupted again on July 12 by alarm guns. His men dropped what they were doing and assembled immediately, muskets ready. They then witnessed the ascent of two British frigates and a few smaller craft up the Hudson River. The British took advantage of a wind from the south and sailed past the American defenses. As the vessels came abreast of each battery of guns on the shore, the American crews fired, and the British returned the fire with their cannon. The thunderous cannonade produced billowing clouds of smoke that rolled up the Hudson, matching the progress of the enemy ships. Each hit on the British ships brought cheers from the American lines; regardless, it soon became abundantly clear that, despite their labor-intensive preparations, the Americans had been unable to stop the British from moving freely along the wide river.[311]

The days grew hot, and the British fleet off New York kept growing. The swelling numbers of British were a constant reminder to officers like Timothy of how titanic the struggle had become. After gazing at the leafless forest of masts anchored to the south, Timothy must have questioned his decision to include his son in this war. With the ever-present danger of British attack looming over the Americans, the soldiers were ordered to sleep with their muskets and prepare to react at a moment's notice.[312] The whole regiment practiced moving in haste from camp to its assigned position in the defenses.[313]

The delirious joy and bravado with which they had received the words of the Declaration of Independence had waned as the men toiled nervously in the heat, and the sobering realization of what still lay ahead tested their resolve. Meanwhile the British fleet had grown to nearly three hundred ships by the middle of July.[314]

The oppressive summer heat and humidity continued to drain the soldiers' energies, driving them to consume more water. Unfortunately, uncontaminated water was in short supply that summer and "camp fever," as dysentery was known, grew to epidemic proportions.[315] Each day, Timothy would record those in his company who were sick and unfit for duty. And those who were too ill were discharged, as was David Moss, from Timothy's company, on July 24.[316] Close to half the American army would become sick that summer. Even Colonel Huntington, as well as over half the Seventeenth Continental Regiment's soldiers, became too ill to perform regular duties.[317] Adding insult to injury, the deadly smallpox virus reappeared, making the dread of death from disease probably greater than the more elusive threat of the augmenting British army.

As the numbers of fit soldiers dwindled around Timothy, the British force grew. Throughout July and into August, the British ships just kept coming; on August 1 a large installment of forty-five new vessels arrived. The first cool day broke a week and a half later, on August 12,[318] bringing some much-needed relief for the soldiers. But that day brought yet another large group of British reinforcements. By then the number of enemy ships visible to the Americans had swelled to over four hundred. This included seventy-three warships, of which eight were ships-of-the-line—colossal vessels with two or more decks of large guns, each complete with hundreds of seamen and at least fifty cannon.[319] It would have been easy for Timothy to calculate that just those eight monsters had close to four times as many cannon as the Americans had in all New York.[320] Clearly the looming contest would prove to be a massive test of resolve for the soldiers of the burgeoning new nation.

The British intended to split the American colonies in two in 1776. They planned to use the historic Hudson River–Lake George–Lake Champlain water highway as the dividing line that would cut off the rebellious New England colonies from the rest and, they hoped, force the insurrection to wither and die. The capture of New York's large harbor was the important initial step towards a proposed union with another British force advancing from Canada. To achieve this goal, the King of England had ordered a massive force to be assembled. General William Howe was appointed commander of the army to assault New York, and his brother, Admiral Richard Howe, would command the naval force. The British army there included twenty-seven regiments of infantry, two battalions of the King's Guard, three brigades of artillery, and one regiment of light dragoon cavalry. In addition, the King had hired eleven regiments of soldiers from small German states in Europe. A large number of them came from the state of Hesse-Kassel. The Hessians, as the Americans dubbed them, were rumored to be fierce, savage foes. Two of the British regiments, the Forty-second and the Seventy-first, were actually Scottish Highlanders. Timothy knew how determined these men could be in a fight after witnessing them in battle in July 1758. Altogether Howe's army numbered about thirty-one thousand.[321] In fact, the British host in New York was the largest oceanic expedition ever dispatched by any European power in the eighteenth century.[322] The British had established camp on Staten Island, southwest across the harbor from New York. Timothy would have seen the smoke rising from the numerous British campfires every day—a constant reminder of the enemy's strength.

The night of August 21 brought a vicious storm, similar to a hurricane. The clouds swirled around the city instead of blowing through like a normal storm. Lightning strikes pounded the area in a cascade, as if the storm itself were impatient and could not wait to unleash the bolts in succession. The whole thing was so intense one could not imagine it would last very long; but the tempest lasted three hours.[323] As the men huddled together in their camps, the storm could easily have been perceived as a sign that the climactic battle of the campaign was fast approaching. Indeed, such fears would have been confirmed the next day as the British moved to attack.

August 22 dawned as a beautiful clear day. The British landed troops on the southwest shore of Long Island with near-perfect precision and drove away the American guards stationed there. The men in Timothy's regiment noticed smoke rising from different points on Long Island late in the morning. About noon, the alarm guns sounded, but Timothy's men had to wait anxiously until four in the afternoon when they received their orders to move immediately to Long Island.[324] The camp burst into frenzied activity. Timothy quickly assembled his company and ordered his officers to check the men's firearms, cartridge boxes, and canteens. Lieutenant Colonel Joel Clark explained the many details of the move to Timothy and the fellow company commanders, and he then dismissed them to carry out the orders. Colonel Huntington was still too ill to command and remained behind.[325]

Timothy's regiment marched down to the harbor and gathered there with several others. As quickly as possible, they loaded onto small boats and shoved off into the East River. The men strained at the creaking oars as they pulled away from the harbor. Governors Island, about a mile to their right, was covered with earthworks and protected their movement on the water. Ahead, rising from the beach, stood the bluffs where Fort Stirling guarded the ferry landing on Long Island. There was a cluster of buildings near the ferry landing, and to the left were more wooded bluffs. After disembarking at the landing, they marched up a road that climbed between the bluffs and, after proceeding about one mile more, the regiment stopped to rest. Here they waited for further orders during which Timothy heard many conflicting reports of the whereabouts of the enemy. One placed the British within two and a half miles of the Americans' current locale, naturally putting the men on edge, while another reported them at a far more secure distance of ten miles.[326]

The men could sense that conflict was imminent and surely struggled with their mounting fears and anxieties. General Washington knew this feeling all too well and hoped to fortify the soldiers' resolve with a commanding statement calling for their steadfastness and recalling the weighty stakes of their engagement. "The hour is fast approaching, on which the honor and success of this army, and the safety of our bleeding country depend," the appeal began. "Remember officers and soldiers that you are free men, fighting for the blessings of liberty—that slavery will be your portion, and that of your posterity, if you do not acquit yourselves like men."[327]

The Seventeenth Continental had been transferred from General Spencer's division in New York and reassigned to the command on Long Island. The reorganization was hampered by recent command changes. General Greene, a well-qualified and resolute commander, had been on Long Island since the beginning of May. He had managed the construction of many of the fortifications and knew the lay of the land very well. Unfortunately, Greene fell ill and was replaced by General Sullivan on August 20. Sullivan had just transferred to New York from the northern campaign in Canada and was altogether unfamiliar with both the troops and the defenses on Long Island.[328]

The confusion caused delays, and Timothy's regiment did not start marching again until after sunset, August 22. The soldiers passed through the small village of Brooklyn with its old Dutch church and followed a road through the earthworks protecting the area from the rest of Long Island. Shortly after exiting the defenses, the column was ordered to halt and the men to load their muskets. Even in the dark Timothy would have seen parts of the massive mile-long earthwork, which included the star-shaped Fort Greene a few hundred yards to the south. And to the north was the Oblong Redoubt positioned close to the road it was intended to help defend. The men stood tensely in the dark. Now they were outside the protection of the fortifications, and no one could be sure there were no British patrols nearby. The march continued for a few miles onto a wooded ridge that overlooked the village of Flatbush. Here the regiment stayed through the rest of the night. Timothy kept his company awake and on guard, lying between the trees.[329]

After the long night without much sleep, the regiment moved forward to the edge of the woods facing Flatbush. Along the road to the town, cannon were positioned to support the Americans.[330] The exhausted and nervous men in Timothy's company waited for daylight, trying to remain calm. Many of them, including Timothy's son, had never faced enemy infantry in battle. As twilight gave way to dawn, Timothy viewed the special German Jager troops, a type of light infantry or riflemen trained to skirmish in rough terrain, below in Flatbush, about a half mile to the south. The green uniforms of the Jagers were very distinct from the red of the British.[331] Flatbush was aptly named, as it sat on a flat plain that stretched out before Timothy. When it became fully light, Timothy's regiment was reinforced by riflemen from Pennsylvania, under the command of Colonel Hand. The Pennsylvanian frontiersmen quickly spread out in front of the Seventeenth Regiment, and advanced to engage the Jagers. Using their long-range rifles, the Pennsylvanians hunted the enemy pickets through the fields and fences below Timothy's position. Timothy's regiment was ordered to wait and support the riflemen if necessary. Timothy watched the Pennsylvanians advance into the village of Flatbush and consequently witnessed their withdrawal under pressure from the German soldiers. Meanwhile, the British moved artillery to Flatbush and began to engage the Americans near Timothy's position. Much of the day was spent playing a deadly game of dodging British cannonballs. After sunset they were relieved by New York soldiers and withdrew further into the woods where they fashioned crude shelters with branches and slept soundly through the night.[332]

At dawn on August 24, the whole regiment was quickly assembled and marched back into the safety of the earthworks around Brooklyn. The men drove some cattle with them that they had collected in order to prevent them falling into the hands of the enemy. The hungry men of Timothy's company were issued food rations, which they prepared and enjoyed for the rest of the day. Cannon sounded in the distance, but since the soldiers were probably used to this now, it did not disturb their day of rest. A number of regiments marched past their position, having come from New York by the ferry. Other regiments left Brooklyn to head out to the wooded ridgeline where the men of the Seventeenth Regiment had been. Even in this relatively safe location the horrors of war remained visible as wounded soldiers passed through their camp, including one with a leg so damaged by a cannonball that in order to save his life it was immediately cut off. The men in Timothy's regiment surely gave thanks for many things that evening while attending a service held by their regimental chaplain in the Brooklyn church, not the least of which was their good fortune in being quartered in a barn and house that evening as they listened to heavy rain pound the roofs over their heads.[333]

The next morning the sound of drums and marching music resounded in Brooklyn as six more regiments approached from the ferry. Among this refortifying column of men was the popular Connecticut General Israel Putnam who had been assigned overall command of the augmenting forces on Long Island. This was the second command change in five days, and even though Putnam was much respected by the soldiers, he, too, was unfamiliar with the land and defenses in the area.[334] At this critical moment in the campaign, this handicap would prove detrimental. Still, that Sunday morning Putnam's arrival uplifted the troops' spirits. He was revered by the men for his bravery and his willingness to endure many of the deprivations of the common soldier. His exploits in the French and Indian War as a Ranger were legendary. Timothy had fought with Putnam against the French and their Indian allies during a fierce skirmish on August 8, 1758, and therefore knew of Putnam's courage and tenacity firsthand. The soldiers' endearing nickname for the General was Old Put.

Timothy's regiment probably missed Putnam's parade into Brooklyn because it had received orders to march forward again and relieve those guarding the wooded ridgeline separating the two armies. Accordingly, the regiment assembled and left Brooklyn at ten o'clock. It passed through the defenses as before, but this time turned right onto the road to Gowanus. This took the men past the large tidal marsh around Gowanus Creek that protected the right flank of the earthwork line at Brooklyn. A small road led to a few buildings around a mill in the middle of the wetlands. The whole marsh covered about a mile of terrain between Brooklyn and Gowanus Bay and formed a perfect natural barrier protecting the right side of the Brooklyn defenses.[335]

Closer to Gowanus Bay, the Seventeenth Regiment assumed its positions, with the wooded ridge on its left. The soldiers faced the British, who controlled a fork in the road where the Red Lion Inn stood. The day was quiet, and the men enjoyed eating the plentiful watermelons in the area. Timothy's men took turns on guard duty, but all they could do was watch the hustle and bustle of the British army and navy on Long Island, Staten Island, and the bay between. A passing rain shower that evening drenched many of their muskets, so the men had to extract the wet powder and clean the barrels to make them serviceable again. They performed this as quickly as possible, hoping the British would not move against them while they were vulnerable. Fortunately, the rest of the night remained quiet.[336]

On Monday, August 26, men in the Seventeenth Regiment collected cattle and other food from the local farms and moved them away from the enemy. In the afternoon they marched back to Brooklyn, but it had become difficult to find lodging in the now-crowded village. The men were forced to stay in any structure they could find; Timothy and the other officers shared rooms.[337]

Timothy awoke before dawn to the boom of signal guns and roused his men in response.[338] They quickly assembled and checked their equipment, all the while many of them surely shivering due to the unseasonable cool temperature.[339] The British had attacked the positions they had left the day before and driven away some militia posted there.[340] General Parsons, the brigade commander for Timothy's regiment, rode briskly out to determine the extent of the British attack, while General Stirling promptly marched three of his regiments, Colonel Smallwood's Maryland, Colonel Haslet's Delaware, and Colonel Atlee's Pennsylvania, to face the enemy. Lieutenant Colonel Clark led Timothy's regiment next, and these men were followed shortly by Lieutenant Colonel Kachlein's Pennsylvania riflemen.[341] As Timothy marched in this large column, other units were scrambling to man the earthworks protecting Brooklyn. All of the American soldiers on Long Island were active. Because many soldiers did not have uniforms, they placed a small branch of pine needles or a twig with leaves in their hats[342] in an effort to differentiate the American soldiers from the local farmers and, more importantly, from those Long Island militia units that had joined the British army. Some of the local militia raised to defend New York had come from communities still loyal to the King, and they had quickly joined the British when they landed on Long Island. These loyalist units were dressed just like the farmers within the American army and were, therefore, impossible to distinguish. Timothy knew from past experience that in the confusion of battle a little bit of green in one's hat might not be noticed, but it was the only practical method they could devise.[343]

General Stirling's column of five regiments reached the advancing British after daylight, and he ordered Atlee's Pennsylvanians to engage the British while continuing to gather his other regiments into a line from the Gowanus road up onto the wooded ridge to the south. Atlee's regiment bravely checked the British advance despite its superior numbers, allowing Stirling enough time to form a defense line.[344] During this time Timothy's regiment moved behind Stirling's line and took position near the crest of a wooded hill to protect the left flank. Atlee's Pennsylvanians then withdrew to join Timothy's regiment on the ridge.

The riflemen in Kachlein's regiment spread out in front of the line to skirmish with the British pickets. Colonel Smallwood's Maryland regiment, some members dressed in their scarlet and buff colored coats, the rest in hunting shirts, guarded the Gowanus road with two artillery pieces. Next in line were the men of Colonel Haslet's Delaware regiment, with their dark-blue coats with red lapels and cuffs.[345] These last two regiments were the best drilled in Washington's army and unlike most were properly uniformed. General Stirling commanded this part of the line. Above Stirling's position were the Seventeenth Continental and Atlee's Pennsylvanians, both under the command of General Parsons. Almost 1,600 Americans proudly faced close to seven thousand British soldiers.[346] There were no earthworks here to protect either side, so the men stood in the open, only their officers' iron will and discipline holding them in place.[347]

The British Fourth Brigade formed in a rectangle configuration alongside the road with two regiments in front, two regiments behind, and two cannon as support. To the south the British Sixth Brigade formed a single line of four regiments, also supported by two cannon. Behind both brigades, in reserve, was the Forty-second Highland Regiment as well as a small force of New York loyalists.[348] This British division was commanded by Major General Grant, who had boasted that he could traverse the American colonies with only five thousand soldiers and that no one could stop him.[349] Yet, on the morning of August 27, some of the best troops in Washington's army faced Grant's force, and they were determined to stop his advance.

The British then advanced to two hundred yards from Stirling's line. This was beyond effective musket range, but from there they could conceivably advance to attack in minutes. The British cannon bombarded the Americans, and the two cannon supporting Stirling returned the fire. Some of the Americans were dramatically decapitated by cannonballs, splattering blood on their neighbors; still the line stood its ground for hours that morning.[350]

Farther up on the wooded ridge, General Parsons commanded close to one hundred in Atlee's regiment and about two hundred in the Seventeeth Regiment.[351] This small force protected General Stirling's left flank. Each of the eight companies in the Seventeenth had, on average, fewer than thirty soldiers,[352] so Timothy could keep a close eye on each of his men and stay near his son. Timothy's battlefield experience probably helped him appear calm, setting a good example for his men. Lieutenant Colonel Clark also held the men together with his presence; like Timothy, he had fought many times in the previous war with the French.[353]

The enemy soon advanced toward them, pushing back some of the American riflemen in front of Timothy's position. As the British got closer, Timothy could see the blue facings on the red uniforms of the Twenty-third Welch Fusiliers Regiment. Next to the Twenty-third marched the red coats with buff facings of the British Fortieth Regiment. Each of these two regiments had more manpower than General Parsons's entire command. Timothy had to make sure his first lieutenant, Nathaniel Gove, and his ensign, Joel Gillet, were both in their correct positions, and to scan his company for anyone not ready. On command, the Americans let loose a hail of lead that brought down a number of the British, including Lieutenant Colonel Grant of the Fortieth Regiment. The Fortieth Regiment's advance ceased under this relentless fire, but the Twenty-third Regiment continued advancing.[354]

Timothy had to encourage his men to keep loading and firing as fast as possible. The gleaming bayonets on the muskets of the attacking Twenty-third Regiment could be seen through the smoke swirling around the trees. The Twenty-third Regiment had been at the Siege of Boston. Some of its men had been at the Battle of Lexington and Concord, as well as fought at Bunker Hill. All of them had suffered from a lack of food and warmth and had felt the shame of withdrawing from Boston in defeat. Six months later it seemed that those past frustrations were now driving the bravery and fortitude of the Welch Fusiliers. Without the support of the Fortieth Regiment they continued forward, taking the full brunt of musket fire from the Americans. Finally, after many of their leaders had fallen, they fell back.[355]

General Parsons's men faced three attacks that morning of August 27, from the Seventeenth, Twenty-third, Fortieth, and Forty-fourth regiments of the British. Yet they held their position and inflicted a large number of casualties on the British. Overall, 130 of Grant's British force were killed or wounded that day, eighty-six of them by Parsons's troops alone, making it evident that the more brutal part of the battle took place around Timothy's regiment.[356] Not only were the troops proud to have defended themselves so well against so much larger an enemy, they also believed—mistakenly, it would turn out—that they had killed the British General Grant. The misinformation spread when someone had found the name Grant in the hat of a fallen man—Lieutenant Colonel Grant of the Fortieth Regiment.[357] Timothy and the men around him felt victorious until, later in the day, circumstances beyond their control worked against them.

The British battle plan called for General Grant to engage General Stirling and General Parsons. Meanwhile, a force of Hessians at Flatbush was to engage those defending on the ridge above the town, while ten thousand more soldiers were to march around the left flank of the Americans. This march started the night before. By nine in the morning the British had reached the town of Bedford, behind the American positions on the wooded ridgeline. This meant this large British force was now behind the forces of General Parsons and General Stirling.[358]

Stirling realized his predicament late in the morning and turned his troops back to face the new threat, only to find the road to Brooklyn blocked by the British. He ordered most of his command to flee across the tidal marsh and Gowanus Creek as best they could while he courageously led a small portion of his brigade in an attack meant to stall the British long enough for the others to escape. Many men were saved, but much of their equipment was abandoned as they struggled through the mud and swam across the creek. General Stirling attacked six times against a force well larger than his own, but he could not break through and was eventually captured.[359]

Unfortunately, General Parsons was not informed that Stirling's force had withdrawn, his gallant three hundred left oblivious on their wooded ridge. They had fought off the British for hours and expended much of their ammunition. Meanwhile, the British had unhinged the defenses along the periphery, and the American line crumbled. This left General Parsons's small force surrounded. These men attempted to move in several directions but had to engage enemy troops wherever they turned.[360] Parsons's tiny command quickly dispersed in the confusion, and many found themselves stuck in a wooded swamp where they decided to split into small groups in hopes of easing their escape.[361]

Timothy and his son were now trapped in a terrifying world, certainly unaware as to what their fate would soon be. No one was sure that the enemy would even take prisoners. Since the issuing of the Declaration of Independence in July, all the American soldiers had become rebels against the King— a crime punishable by death. Perhaps execution would be in store for those Americans captured by the British. The uncertainty fueled their fears. Throughout the area of the battlefield there were scores of tiny groups, sometimes even single men, all desperately searching for escape. Some were hysterical, claiming to have witnessed the Hessians bayoneting men after they surrendered, pinning them to trees.[362] Others hid in swamps or thick stands of trees and eventually reached the American lines. Timothy and his son were not so lucky and were captured. It is highly likely that they suffered from physical and verbal abuse from their captors. They were marched to a house and barn close to where they started the action with the British in the morning. Crowded into the barn were many other prisoners from different regiments, but Timothy soon found familiar faces from the Seventeenth Regiment.[363] Most of his regiment was captured, including twenty-five from Timothy's company. One of Timothy's sergeants, Rous Bly, had died. With the exception of those who had been too sick and were left behind in New York, the Seventeenth Continental Regiment ceased to exist.[364] The prisoners shared accounts of the taunts and the stones thrown at them after their surrender. They also were horrified by the extreme case of Captain Joseph Jewett, who had been bayoneted while trying to surrender, and was left with two agonizing wounds, one in the breast and another in his belly.[365] And it was not until morning that the British could spare a surgeon to dress and attend to those wounded prisoners.[366]

On August 28 the situation improved somewhat. Some British officers did begin to treat the prisoners with respect and provided a meal of mutton. General Grant ordered his servant to prepare the meal, which was much appreciated since it had been over twenty-four hours since the prisoners had last eaten. Still, Captain Jewett's condition worsened all day. Lieutenant Jabez Fitch stayed with his captain all that night and took his last requests. The captain struggled with the pain until early the next morning when he finally died. He was buried later that day in an orchard close by. Heavy rains poured, adding to the depressing scene at the graveside.[367]

Around four in the afternoon, all the officers and most of the soldiers had been gathered together and marched down to the shore, where they were made to wade through two hundred yards of mud in order to get deep enough in the water to be loaded onto small craft. At this point Timothy and the officers were separated from the men and loaded on one boat, while the others, with their hands tied, were put into other craft. Then they were rowed out into the enormous fleet in the harbor. Certainly, Timothy anxiously tried to keep track of his son. Rain continued to douse the prisoners. As they passed some of the British vessels, those on board further chastised them with insults. Near Staten Island they were transferred to the India-class merchant vessel the *Pacific*, which was a large three-masted transport containing supplies, including artillery carriages, lumber, and rigging for sail. The nearly four hundred prisoners were herded down below deck by abusive guards. By the time all the soaked, muddy men had traipsed through the lower decks, the floors had become covered with sloppy goo that reached halfway up everyone's shoes. And it was here that they were forced to spend the night, each trying to find a place to curl up amid the muck and equipment. So many prisoners were crammed into the vessel that only half could lie down at one time. Timothy reunited with his son, and they struggled to rest.[368]

They spent the next two days on the *Pacific*. The water provided to them was considered unfit for livestock, and the food was not much better. The ship's crew and the guards overseeing the prisoners hurled insults regularly and spread stories of American defeat and threats of rebel death sentences. On the morning of September 1, all the prisoners were transferred onto another ship, the *Lord Rochford*. The new vessel was about half the size of the *Pacific*, but the prisoners were allowed access to more areas, so the overcrowding conditions actually remained about the same. Timothy and the other officers were held on the open quarterdeck of the *Lord Rochford*. The open air was certainly better than the choking stench below decks, but they were left exposed to the weather.[369]

Near sunset on September 3, more prisoners were placed on another vessel, the *Mentor*, alongside the *Lord Rochford*. The *Mentor* was a two-masted, snow-class vessel with square sails and an auxiliary mast behind the mainmast that carried a trysail. It was soon discovered that Lieutenant Colonel Clark, as well as other officers from the Seventeenth Regiment, were among the captives on the *Mentor*. The next morning, a number of the officers were allowed to transfer to the *Mentor* to visit their comrades held there. The men captured by the Hessians recounted many incidents of physical abuse, including being beaten with the butts of muskets and having money, personal possessions, shoes, and clothing stolen. One soldier from the Seventeenth, Samuel Tallman, was reportedly used as a target for musket practice by his captors and received two wounds, one in the neck and one in the arm.[370]

Timothy was busy caring for his son, who had suffered horribly under the unhealthy conditions of the prison ships and had fallen ill. Treating his son's fever without proper food or water was impossible, but Timothy struggled to do his best. His son was not the only one requiring special attention; many on board were suffering from wounds or were sick. The dark lower deck of the prison ship contained not only the multitude of men in filthy clothes but also buckets full of their excrement, soiled makeshift bandages from infected wounds, and the overpowering odor that accompanied it all. The days and nights dragged on during which time Timothy's son failed to get better. Making matters even worse, the officers were all moved to the *Mentor* on the evening of September

5, separating them from the men on the *Lord Rochford* and Timothy from his ailing son.[371]

Finally, on the afternoon of September 6, Timothy was given permission to take his son ashore to a hospital for better care. A storm brewed that evening, and rain pelted the area, surely making it difficult for Timothy to find a dry place for his suffering son in the hospital full of more wounded and sick. While there, Timothy learned from another prisoner that General Parsons had evaded capture and rejoined the army, but very few from his tiny brigade had escaped death or capture.[372] Timothy tended to his son for days with limited resources, but to his utter devastation, young Timothy slowly withered away and soon died.[373]

Timothy was probably Captain Percival's firstborn, but a lack of birth records prevents a definite determination. In any event, the loss of Timothy Jr. would have broken Timothy's spirit. And the fact that he could not share the loss with Mary made it that much harder and surely intensified the grief both suffered.

Timothy returned to the *Mentor* on September 10 and remained there in the miserable conditions until October 7. While on board, he witnessed the huge fire that consumed much of New York City on September 21. This occurred shortly after the British occupied the town, and was believed to have been ignited by supporters of the rebellion. When a large number of the prisoners were transferred to the city on October 7, Timothy was able to survey much of the damage from the inferno. He was lodged in a building close to Broadway, and was allowed to move about the city during the day. Unlike the officers, the soldiers were confined to large contaminated buildings where the living conditions closely resembled those aboard the prison ships. During this period Timothy's daily concerns revolved around finding enough food for himself and his men, hoping for an exchange of prisoners that might grant him his freedom, and acquiring any further news of the ongoing war.[374]

As new prisoners came into the city, Timothy would hear bits and pieces of news, such as that of the American forces' retreat from the city and the ensuing Battle of White Plains on October 28. On November 16, the British attacked and captured Fort Washington north of the city. This brought close to three thousand new prisoners into the already cramped holding places in New York.[375] While these new captives brought with them much desired news, they also strained the resources of the British to care for them, and food became even scarcer.[376]

The British policy was to supply the prisoners with rations equal to two-thirds of what their own soldiers received. Yet the American officers discovered that their men sometimes did not even receive half of what they were due. Moreover, the men would sometimes get nothing for days at a time. What they did receive would often be rotten and moldy. Keeping himself and his men properly clothed, warm, and fed had to become Timothy's prime concern. This task was made even more difficult because the officers were often prevented from seeing and talking to the men; British guards would sometimes chase them away with fixed bayonets or drawn swords, sometimes even beating them with canes.[377]

The men suffered from wounds, starvation, and disease. Their clothes became tattered, rotten rags covered with vermin. Just as he had helplessly watched his son die, Timothy saw other captive soldiers quickly fade into skeletal forms with pale skin and glazed, sunken eyes. John Moody, from Timothy's company, died late in November or early December.[378] Their brave Lieutenant Colonel Clark perished from disease on December 16.[379] Death took men away almost daily; just as a dying candle struggles to keep aflame, hope for a reprieve barely flickered for the thousands confined in and around New York.

Timothy and most of the officers from the Seventeenth Regiment were moved to the community of Long Lots, Long Island, in January 1777. They were housed in people's homes throughout the village that bordered a salt marsh on the shore of the Atlantic. Here their physical conditions improved, but they lost contact with their men still trapped in the dungeon-like conditions in New York and on the prison ships.[380]

At some point during his captivity, Timothy's wife, Mary, made the long trip from Chatham, Connecticut, to New York. She packed food, warm clothes, and medicine, and attempted to deliver them personally. But no amount of pleading or bribery could shake the British commander from his firm stance that no one was allowed to see the prisoners. Mary had to turn back, disheartened, and return home.[381]

When news reached the prisoners at Long Lots of the decisive American victory at Saratoga, New York, in October of 1777, Timothy gained renewed hope of finally being freed.[382] The Americans had captured over three thousand British soldiers,[383] and it was expected that exchanges would be forthcoming. By December, many officers headed home at last;[384] unfortunately, Timothy was not one of them. He languished in captivity until his release on May 15, 1778. It was not until late in May that he finally arrived home.[385] Memories of his long, difficult service would likely haunt him for some time to come. Timothy survived twenty-one forlorn months as a prisoner of war. Part of that period he suffered under the most dire of conditions and circumstances, the terrible, premature death of his son certainly being the worst. When Timothy was at long last reunited with Mary, one hopes that, for a moment, the horrors of his arduous service and captivity faded from the grips of his memory.

Epilogue

Timothy stayed home less than two months before reentering the armed struggle that both he and Mary firmly believed needed him again. On July 8, 1778, the Connecticut Assembly appointed the experienced Captain Percival to replace another captain who had been excused from serving in the state militia that summer. Timothy commanded a militia company sent to the New London area of Connecticut to defend the important harbor.[386] Later in August, he served for a short time with the militia in operations around Newport, Rhode Island.[387]

The British had occupied Newport since December 1776 because it was a valued harbor for their fleet. In August 1778 the Americans planned to capture Newport with the help of their new ally, France. The French had committed twelve ships-of-the-line, four frigates, and four thousand soldiers to this operation. Due to a number of events, including a storm that damaged many French ships and the arrival of a British fleet, the French departed in the middle of the operation.

Timothy probably wondered if his old enemy from the last war could ever have become a valuable ally in the current struggle. Without French assistance, the attack on the British defenses at Newport was impractical and, therefore, cancelled. On August 29, the British advanced against the American army outside of Newport and met them in battle. It is not clear if Timothy served with the five hundred militiamen present at this battle, but it is clear he survived and returned home.

Finally, Timothy was able to concentrate on his family again, and on the operation of his farm in Chatham. Yet the war effort remained close to the hearts of both Timothy and Mary. He was a local leader in the effort to raise equipment and supplies for the American army.[388] Mary turned her home into a makeshift hospital serving the needs of any soldier in the area. The wounded, sick, hungry, and cold were all welcome. Mary and her daughters used homemade medicines to treat the poor veterans, including a soothing bread-dough concoction on the frostbitten or blistered, bleeding feet of the soldiers. Many worn and shoeless men left the Percival home with feet bound in whatever material could be spared and a good meal in their bellies.[389]

Timothy and Mary even had another son whom they again named Timothy. This second Timothy could not completely replace the loss of their first, but they surely hoped the new Timothy would live his life without suffering the experiences of warfare.

At some point before 1790, Timothy and Mary left Chatham and moved to Freehold, New York, with Timothy Jr. and their youngest daughter, Lydia.[390] It seems that Timothy's younger brother, Paul, and his family joined them there as well. In addition, two of Timothy's daughters, Mary and Anna, moved to Freehold with their families. Mary had married John Palmer, and Anna had married Levi Stedman.[391]

In later years, Timothy and Mary's two other sons also moved to Freehold. Elkanah, named after Mary's father, brought his wife, and Jabez transported his wife, Elizabeth, and their four children from Marlborough, Massachusetts, between

1792 and 1794. There in Freehold, southwest of Albany, the lives of the Percivals became intertwined with the Tousey family. Three Tousey brothers—Thomas, Moses, and Zerah, also from Connecticut—had settled in Freehold as well. Timothy and Mary's youngest daughter, Lydia, soon married Thomas Tousey. On November 17, 1797, Jabez Percival even named his newborn son Zerah Tousey Percival in recognition of the close family ties.[392]

During the last years of the eighteenth century, many people of the new nation of the United States of America migrated to the Ohio River Valley area. Vast tracts of inexpensive land were made available for settlement in what was called the Indiana Territory, which incorporated the current states of Ohio, Indiana, Michigan, Illinois, and Wisconsin. Many of those searching for a new life hauled their families over rugged roads in Pennsylvania to Fort Pitt, in present-day Pittsburgh. From there they traveled down the Ohio River in flat-bottomed boats resembling wooden rafts. Although most of the hostile Indians had been pushed out of the area, there were still some Indians left who preyed upon the settlers floating down the Ohio River. The lure of more land outweighed the danger of Indian attack for most, and streams of people flooded into the area.[393]

The vision of a fresh start on the virgin soil of the Ohio River Valley captivated a number of Percivals and Touseys. Jabez Percival was the first to move his family during the years 1801 and 1802. He was one of the first settlers to construct a log house in what would become the town of Lawrenceburg, along the north bank of the Ohio River, in what would become the state of Indiana. This frontier community was located in Dearborn County, adjacent to Ohio, about thirty miles west of Cincinnati. When the Indiana Territory was organized in 1803, he was appointed judge for Dearborn County and would hear common pleas and handle local matters to uphold the peace. Court was held in Jabez's cabin and, like many frontier courts lacking proper facilities, was an unceremonious affair where practical judgments were used to solve unique problems. Jabez had studied to be a doctor, and he served the area residents with his medical skills as well. He developed a fine reputation as one willing to care for anybody, anytime, day or night.[394]

In 1803, the Tousey brothers—Thomas, Moses, and Zerah—made the long journey with their families as well, and settled just across the river from Jabez in Kentucky. Following the Touseys was George Whitman Percival, a nephew of Timothy's and brother of Moses's wife. They created their own community named Touseytown.[395] They built their homes on a beautiful hilly section overlooking the Ohio River, near where Jacob Piatt was finishing a large house that would be known as Federal Hall. The Piatt family had moved there in 1795 and owned a number of ferries in the area.[396] Thomas Tousey soon took over the operation of the Piatt ferry below Touseytown that connected with Lawrenceburg. He also ran a tavern near the ferry.[397]

By 1807, Timothy Percival, Jr., had left Freehold, New York, to follow his sisters to Touseytown.[398] This meant that Timothy and Mary were left in Freehold, New York, with few of their grandchildren and relatives around. Their longing to be with more family members may have driven them to also make the arduous journey to Touseytown after 1810.[399] There they spent the last few years of their lives with two of their children and sixteen grandchildren. And it was only a short ferry ride across the Ohio River to Lawrenceburg to the home of a third child and six more grandchildren. The large extended family provided a wonderful setting, where family legend indicates they would gather to retell the events of the French and Indian War and the War of Independence.[400]

Timothy and Mary had endured many trials during those two wars. Timothy had struggled through all types of weather conditions, from hot, humid summers that sapped one's strength to frigid winter days trudging through snow or freezing mud that numbed the feet and limbs. He survived grueling wilderness campaigns hauling equipment through forbidding forests, fighting French soldiers, ambushing Indians, not to mention coping with the incessant problems of relentless biting insects and deadly diseases. Throughout this tumultuous experience, Timothy earned the respect of his peers and promotions in military rank. During Timothy's absence, Mary persevered, meeting the daunting challenges of running the family farm and raising their children. With grit and determination, they both outlasted the tests of the French and Indian War only to have another conflict subsequently tear apart their lives again in 1775. In a true test of their resolve, they wholeheartedly entered the War of Independence, willingly enduring many of the same deprivations all over again. Not only did they suffer as individuals, they also sacrificed their son to the cause. Still, despite this greatest of personal losses, Timothy and Mary were unwavering in their support for the cause of their emerging new nation. In many ways the Percivals' story represents what thousands of New England families experienced—common folk facing the myriad trials of this transformative era with undying courage.

There on the frontier of the growing nation, Timothy died on June 16, 1815, and Mary followed on March 12, 1819.[401] They are probably buried in the old Touseytown graveyard overlooking the Ohio River, but no gravestones have been found to indicate as much. By the end of the War of 1812, Timothy had lived through four wars fought on the American continent[402] and had bravely fought in two of them. The last war was referred to at the time as the Second War of Independence; its outcome assured the world that the fledgling nation would survive as an independent country. Timothy therefore died believing that his children, their children, and many generations to come could thrive from the many fruits of freedom for which his service had been so boldly committed.

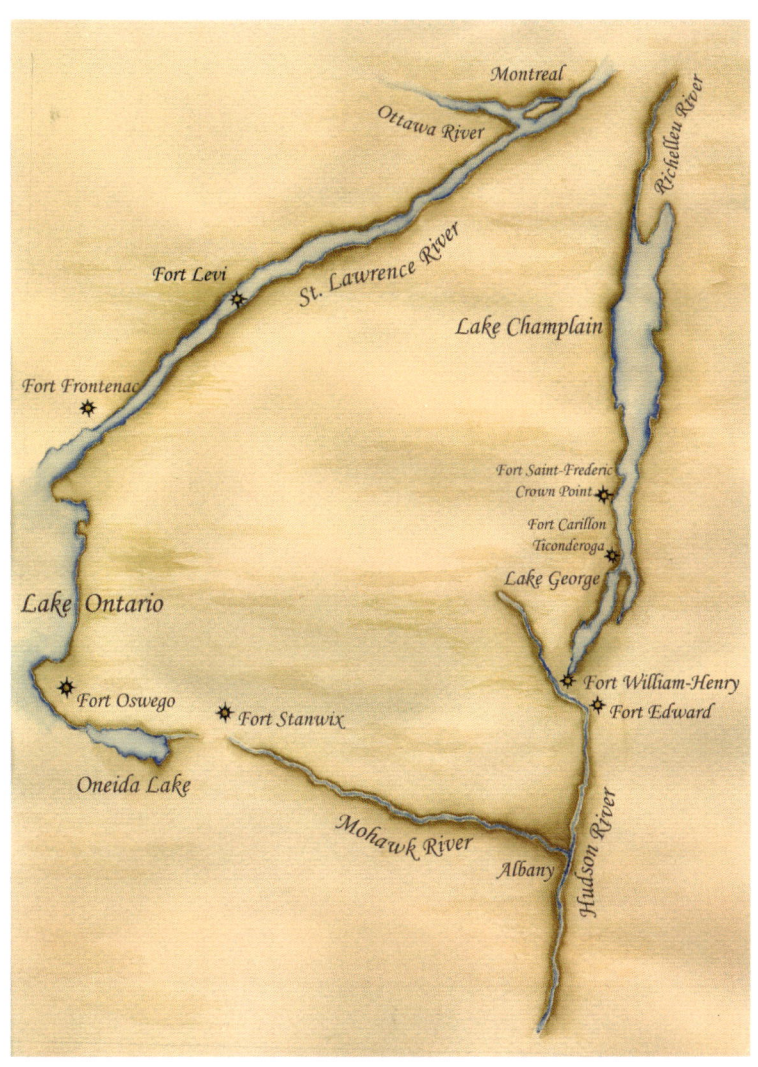

French & Indian War Campaign Area - 1755–1760

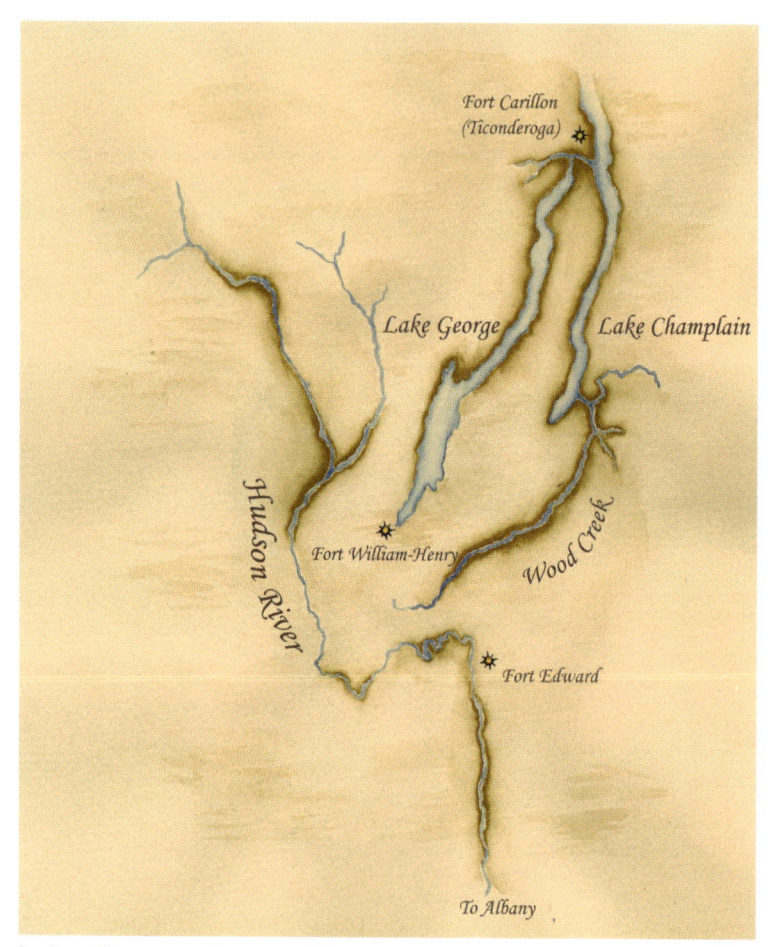

Lake George Area - 1755

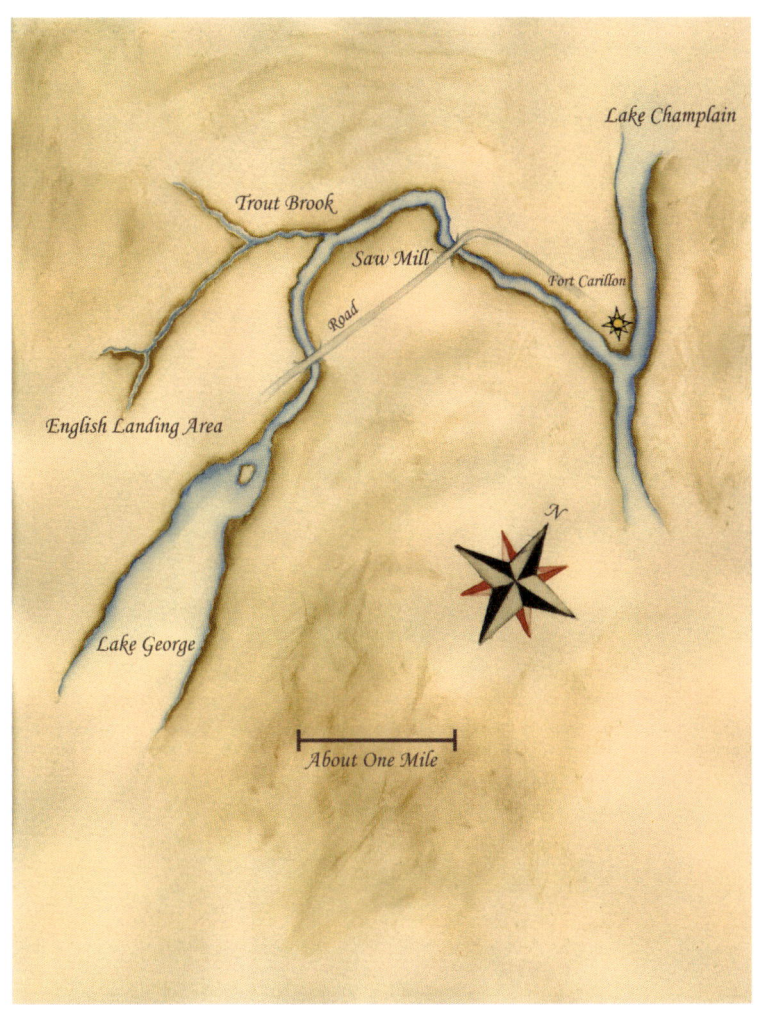

Area between Lake George and Fort Carillon - July 1758

DANIEL D. KINLEY

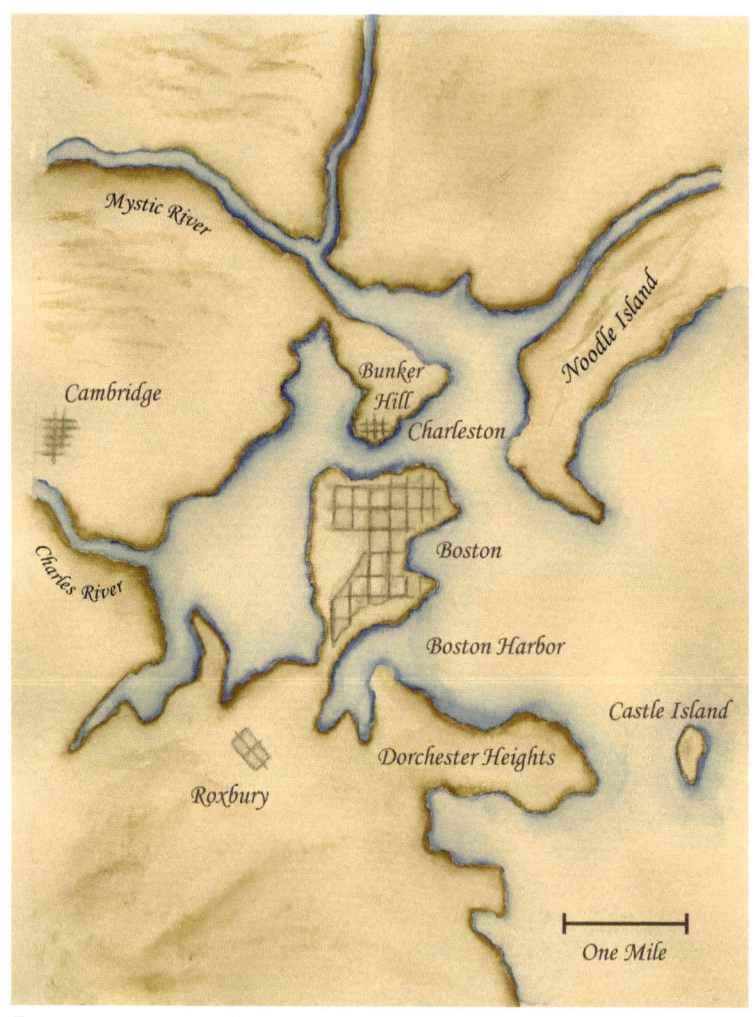

Boston Area - 1775

COMMON COURAGE

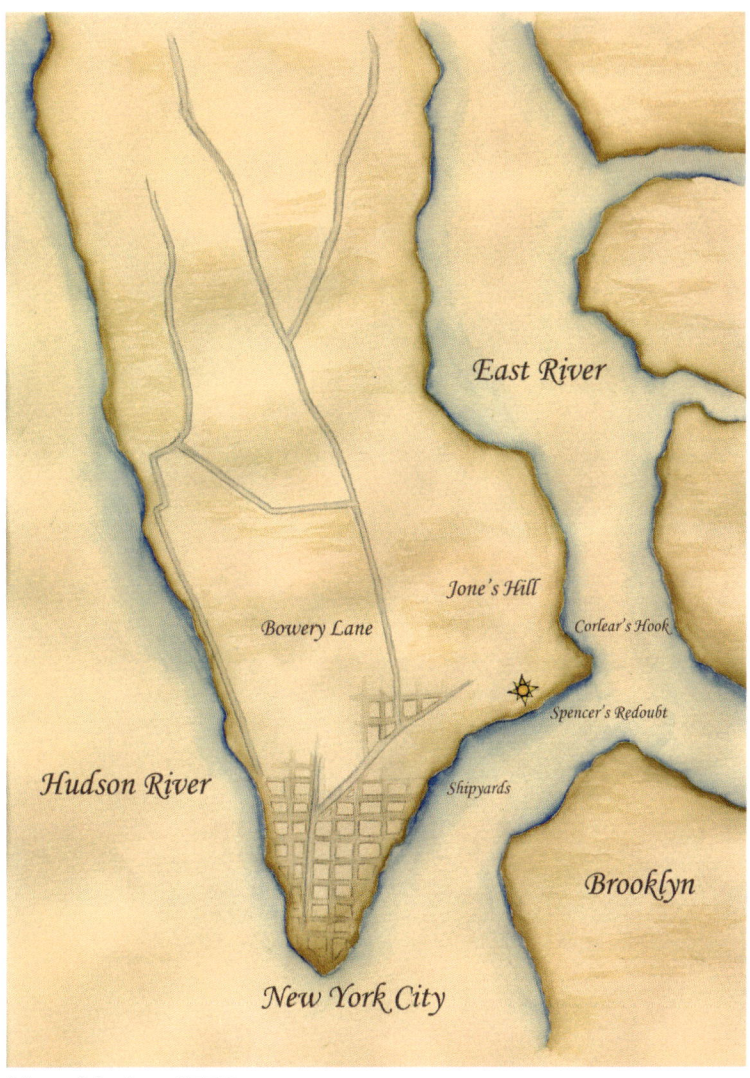

New York - 1776

DANIEL D. KINLEY

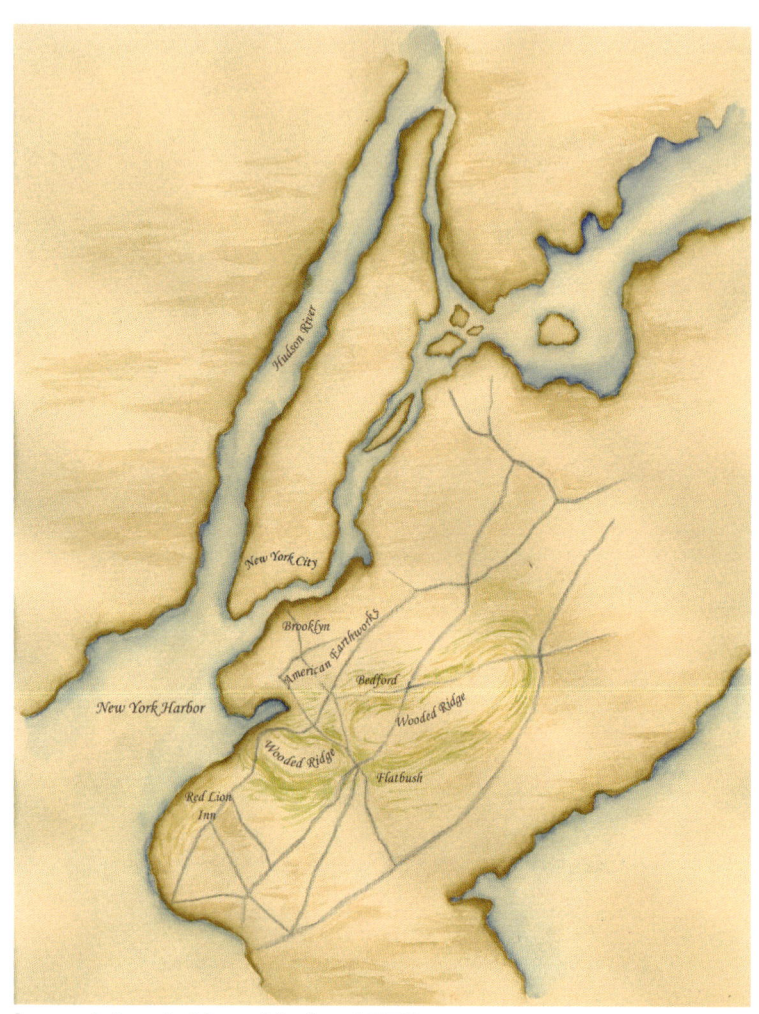

Long Island, New York - 1776

APPENDIX A

Muster lists of the military companies in which Timothy Percival served during the French and Indian War

1755 Campaign: Captain Samuel Dimock's Company

Capt. Samuel Dimock
Lt. Christopher Helms
Lt. Benjamin King
Sgt. Thomas Drinkwater
Sgt. Elisha Kartland
Sgt. Allen Leet
Sgt. Benjamin Woodworth
Clerk John Griswould
Corp. Elliab Farnam
Corp. Jabez Howland
Corp. Timothy Percival
Drum. Nathanial Hall
Simon Bagonet
Andrew Baldwin
Samuel Bennet
Increase Billings
Samuel Bolden
Edward Bostrick
William Brown
Peter Buck
William Button
Samuel Cabel
Samuel Camfield
Henry Chip
John Chopts
Roger Clark
Cornelius Coen
Andrew Coley
Daniel Comstock
Ebenezar Crosby
Christopher Crouck
Samuel Cummins
Andrew Currecompt
George Dibel
Nathanial Divine
Richard Dorus
Stephen Downer
Zebulon Dudley
John Ergetstone
Moses Fisher
Nathan Fisher
Benjamin Flagg
David Franklin
Edward Fuller
Ellisha Gard
Thomas Graves
Cornelius Hannaball
Benjamin Harrak
Samuel Hudson
John Indian
Archabel Johnson
Thomas Lamb
Calvin Leavenworth
William Lord
John Loveland
Samuel Mack
William Markham
Zephaniah Michel
Isack Molatt
Joseph Mosely
Elihu Palmer
Charles Pawheagg
Ebenezer Pelton
William Perigoo
Jacob Pompey
Tafett Pompey
Robert Powe
Samuel Rament
Samuel Renols
Samuel Reves
Joshua Rogers
Gershom Rowley
Israel Rowley
Reuben Rousk
Reben Rusk
Daniel Sejrus
John Shaw
Charles Sharper
Thomas Shearman
Elliakim Spencer
Jabez Spencer
Stephen Spencer
Zacheus Still
Francis Summers
John Tacker

DANIEL D. KINLEY

Samuel Teall
Joseph Toley
Samuel Toodd
Samuel Tooley
Christopher Tooly

Chareuel Toucy
Robben Toucy
John Towump
James Warner
Jonathan Washbone

Thomas Webb
John Wetmore
Boaz Williams
John Ycout

1756 Campaign: Capt. Edmund Wells's Company, Fourth Connecticut Regiment

Capt. Edmund Wells
Lt. Daniel Cone
Lt. John Kilborn
Sgt. Orlando Mack
Sgt. Timothy Percival
Sgt. Pollicarpos Smith
Sgt. Ebenezer Sumner
Clerk Thomas Sumner
Corp. Isaac Goodell
Corp. John Harris
Corp. Zep(?) Mitchell
Corp. Jabue Strong
Drum. Isaac Bigelow
Ancel Annable
Joshua Baly
John Brown
Nathanial Brown
Bar(?) Brainard
Thomas Brewer
Thomas Carrier
Silvanas Cone
Calab Cook
William Cox
Hosea Curtice
John Curtice

Joseph Davis
David Dean
Jeremy Dinney
Isaac Dunham
Labeas Eddy
Samuel Feilding
Nathanial Fisher
John Foord
Garsham Fox
Lemuel Fox
Samuel Fox
Samuel Fox Jr.
William Fox
Eli Gay
Henry Gray
John Gilbord
John Holdrig
Moses Hutchinson
Jarad Knowlton
Roswell Knowlton
Abner Mack
Samuel Mack
John Mitchell
Joseph Mitchell
Nethanial Moot

James Noble
Benjamin Ollcot
Timothy Osborn
Uzziel Owen
Isaac Robin
Isaac Robin Jr.
Gersam Rowlee
Henry Smith
Isaac Smith
Ellekem Spencer
Levis Tattinton
Joseph Taylor
Joseph Taylor Jr.
Nathanial Taylor
Benjamin Tucker
Joseph Tuttill
Samuel Warters
William Warters
Timothy Waters
Levi Webstor
Benjamin West
John West
Nathanial Wickwier
Solomon Wickwier

1757 Alarm Company for the Relief of Fort William Henry

Capt. Daniel Cone
Lt. John Chamberlin
Lt. John McCall
Ens. Ephraim Fuller
Sgt. Eleazer Braynard
Sgt. John Church
Sgt. Timothy Percival
Sgt. William Welch

Clerk Stephen Gardner
Corp. Elija Ackly
Corp. William Doge
Corp. Benjamin Fuller
Corp. Daniel Warner
Drum. Elija Kilborn
Abraham Ackley
Nathanial Ackley

William Akins
Nathan Beebe
Elisha Beckwith
Jo(?) Beckwith
James Bogue
Elishil Booge
Jo(?) Borden
Jared Braynard

136

COMMON COURAGE

Thomas Brooks
John Chamberlin
Elisha Chapman
Jonah Chapman
Stephen Chapman
Ruben Cone
Thomas Cone
James Cook
Ezekiel Crocker
Samuel Dodge
Daniel Emmons
James Forsyth
Daniel Fuller
Levi Gates
Timothy Gates
Jonathan Gilbert
Sterling Graves
John Hambleton

Jonathan Harris
Christopher Holmes
John Hungerford
Lem(?) Hungerford
Asa Jones
Thomas Knowlton
William Markhum
Edmund Marsh
Christopher Minor
Thomas Northam
Benjamin Olcott
Rufus Randel
James Ransome
James Rogers
Arter Scovel
Michael Scovel
John Shaw
John Sheperson

Ebenezer Smith
James Sparrow
Fredrick Spencer
Stephen Spencer
Alex Stewart
Isaac Tatton
Ashel Taylor
Nathanial Taylor
John Tenant
Deliverence Waters
Thomas Webb
David Willey
Lem(?) Willey
Daniel Williams
Hez(?) Usher
Silv(?) Youngs

1758 Campaign: Maj. Spencer's Company, Second Connecticut Regiment

Maj. Joseph Spencer
Lt. Daniel Brainard
Lt. Israel Harding
Ens. Timothy Percival
Sgt. Zephariah Andrews
Sgt. Benjamin Fuller
Sgt. James Sparrow
Sgt. Jonathan Spencer
Clerk Stephen Gardner
Corp. William Aken
Corp. Abner Scovel
Corp. Micah Scovel
Corp. Ephriam Tiffany
Drum. Lem(?) Harding
Drum. Joshua Isham
Nathanial Ackley
Nicolas Ackley
Samuel Ackley
Ansel Anable
John Avory
John Baits
Thomas Baker
Elisha Beckwith
Nathan Beebe
James Booge

Richard Booge
David Brooks
James Brooks
Nathan Burnam
Daniel Chapman
Solomon Chapman
Jonathon Chappel
Uriah Church
Thomas Cocks
Benjamin Cone
George Cone
Joshua Cone
Caleb Cook
Ebenezer Cook
James Cook
Ezekiel Crocker
Amos Dodge
John Dodge
Moses Dodge
Thomas Dodge
Joseph Ernold
Joseph Fox
Joshua Fox
Oliver Fox
Samuel Fox

Samuel Fox Jr.
Daniel Gates
John Gilbert
Mark Graves
Thomas Graves
Henry Gray
John Green
Jared Griswold
Asa Harris
Ezra Harvey
Thomas Harvey
Christopher Holmes
Thomas Holmes
Ebenezer Horton
Samuel Horton
Samuel Hun
Solomon Mack
William Markham
Barnard (Barnebas)
   Phelps May
Jacob Miller
Andrew Minard
Pierce Mobb
John Phelps
Elias Purple

137

Mathew Ransom
Benjamin Reed
Samuel Reed
Elisha Robbens
Gershom Rowley
John Ryant
Simeon Sanders
Henry Scovel
Thomas Shepard

James Smith
John Smith
Fredrick Spencer
Joel Spencer
Joseph Spencer
Zaccheus Spencer
Benjamin Stark
David Stocker
Reuben Tatson

Isaac Tatton
Caleb Tennant
Abraham Warner
Stephen Whittlesy
Samuel Willey
Zacchariah William

1760 Campaign: Lt. Col. Spencer's Company, Second Connecticut Regiment

Lt. Col. Joseph Spencer
Lt. Timothy Percival
Lt. Levi Wells
Ens. James Sparrow
Sgt. Benjamin Brooks
Sgt. Christopher Holmes
Sgt. John Hungerford
Sgt. Jonathon Spencer
Clerk George Griffing
Corp. Arthar Ackley
Corp. Nathan Burnam
Corp. Stephen Otis
Corp. Ebenezer Smith
Drum. Zaccheus Spencer
Drum. John Whitmore
Jeremiah Ackley
Samuel Ackley
Silas Ackley
Zeph(?) Andrews
Elijah Bailey
Ichabod Bailey
John Barley
Nathan Beebe
Richard Beebe
Roswill Beebe
Samuel Beebe
Cyrus Beekwith

William Bibben
James Booge
James Booge Jr.
John Bote
Ebenezer Chapman
Samuel Church
Uriah Church
Caleb Cook
John Cook
Eliezer Cone
Ephram Day
Elias Dewey
Rufus Dewey
Martin Dible
Alexander Dodge
Daniel Dridps
Amasa Fox
Israel Fox
David Fuller
Daniel Gates
Ezra Gates
James Glass
Elea(?) Graves
John Harvey
Thomas Harvey
Daniel Hill
Samuel Hines
Thomas Holmes
Joshua Hurlbut

Daniel Mackall
Joseph Markam
William Markam
Lemuel Marsh
Samuel Mitchel
Zeph Mitchel
George Parker
Joseph Parker
Barnard Phelps
Ezekiel Ransom
Robart Ransom
Daniel Rathbon
Benjamin Reed
Elijah Robens
Benjamin Scovel
Eph(?) Scovel
John Sheparson
Lemuel Shirtleff
Joseph Skinner
Hobart Spencer
Jeremiah Spencer
Simion Spencer
Zachariah Spencer
Isaac Tatten
John Trible
Mathew Warler
Henry Waterus
John Whitne

APPENDIX B

August 27, 1776, Seventeenth Continental Regiment Casualty List, Battle of Long Island

FIELD OFFICERS & STAFF

Lt. Colonel Joel Clark	prisoner
Surgeon's Mate Silas Holmes	prisoner
Adjutant Elisha Hopkins	prisoner
Quartermaster Thomas Fanning	prisoner

CAPTAINS

Ebenezer Fitch Bissell	prisoner
Ozias Bissell	prisoner
Jonathan Brewster	prisoner
Joseph Jewett	prisoner and mortally wounded
Timothy Percival	prisoner
Caleb Trowbridge	prisoner

FIRST LIEUTENANTS

Jabez Fitch	prisoner
Jonathan Gillet	prisoner
Nathaniel Gove	prisoner
Solomon Orcutt	prisoner

SECOND LIEUTENANTS

Solomon Makepeace	prisoner

DANIEL D. KINLEY

ENSIGNS

Anthony Bradford   prisoner
Joseph Chapman   prisoner
Joel Gillet   prisoner
Cornelius Higgins   prisoner
John Kinsman   prisoner
Elihu Lyman   prisoner and wounded

ENLISTED MEN [(K)=killed, (M)=missing]

Capt. Tyler's company
Joseph Arnold (M)
Reuben Bates (M)
Jonathan Barnard (M)
Azariah Benton (M)
Elisha Benton (M)
Josiah Benton (M)
Luke Kimball (M)
Bartlett Lewis (M)
Lemuel Lewis (M)
James Lindsey (M)
Olive Jennings (M)
Seth Rider (M)
John Smith (M)
Jeremiah Sparks (M)
Jesse Swaddle (M)
Joseph White (M)
Jonathan Witherd (M)

Capt. Jewett's company
Joshua Blake (M)
Jasper Briffin (M)
Rufus Cone (M)
Billa Dyer (M)
Peleg Edwards (M)
William Eluther (M)
Theophilus Emerson (M)
Roswel Graves (M)
Elisha Miller (M)
Adam Mitchel (M)
Stephen Ottis (M)
Charles Phelps (M)
Silas Phelps (M)
Zadock Pratt (M)
Nathan Raymond (M)
Eliphalet Reynolds (M)
Oliver Rude (M)
Ebenezer Smith (M)
Jacob Sterling (M)
Timothy Tiffany (M)
Rufus Tracy (M)
Peter Way (M)
Lebbeus Wheeler (M)
Duroy Whittlesey (M)
Nathan Wood (M)
David Yerrington (M)

Capt. Trowbridge's company
William Bedlock (M)
Silas Bottom (M)
Alexander Brine (M)
Joseph Clarke (M)
John Colegrove (M)
Luke Durfee (M)
Daniel Farnam (M)
Levi Farnham (M)
George Foster (M)
George Gordon (M)
John Gardner (M)
Caleb Green (M)
Daniel Ingalls (M)
Ebenezer Keyes (M)
John Kingsbury (M)
Robert Lithgow (M)
Benjamin Lownsbury (M)
Daniel Malone (M)
Solomon Mears (M)
Ishmael Moffit (M)
Joseph Mursur (M)
John Pollard (M)
Stephen Potter (M)
Allen Richards (M)
Joseph Russell (M)
David Saunders (M)
Monday Smith (M)
Moses Smith (M)
John Talmage (M)
John Thomas (M)
William Turner (M)
Samuel White (M)
John Winter (M)

Capt. Ozias Bissell's company
Nathan Barney (M)
Abner Belding (M)
Freegrace Billings (M)
Daniel Church (M)
Lemuel Deming (M)
George Edwards (M)

Thomas Green (M)
Jesse Judson (M)
David Lindsey (M)
Joseph A. Minot (M)
Michael Mitchel (M)
Howard Moulton (M)
Samuel Moulton (M)
Giles Nott (M)
James Price (M)
Jonathan Price (M)
Benjamin Ripnor (M)
Timothy Risley (M)
Joel Skinner (M)
Daniel Thomas (M)
Robert Wallas (M)
Ebenezer Wright (M)

Capt. Brewster's company
Simon Armstrong (M)
Jabez Avery (M)
Jesse Barnett (M)
William Button (M)
Joseph Ellis (M)
Asa Fox (M)

Samuel Fuller (M)
Elijah Hammond (M)
Sanford Herrick (M)
Theophilus Huntingtun (M)
Solomon Huntley (M)
Luther Japhet (M)
John Lewis (M)
Thomas Matterson (M)
Roger Packard (M)
Rufus Parke (M)
Jehiel Pettis (M)
Amasa Pride (M)
Samuel Tallman (M)
John Vandeusen (M)
Calvin Waterman (M)
John Williams (M)

Capt. Percival's company
Samuel Agard (M)
Daniel Bartholomew (M)
Silas Bates (M)
Rous Bly (K)
John Bray (M)
Solomon Carrington (M)
Roger Coit (M)
John Curtis (M)
John Dutton (M)
Daniel Freeman (M)
Gad Fuller (M)
Abel Hart (M)
Jason Hart (M)
Uriah Hungerford (M)
Timothy Isham (M)
Azariah Lothrop (M)
John Moody (M)
Timothy Percival (M)
Isaac Potter (M)
Jesse Roberts (M)
Elijah Rose (M)
Elijah Stanton (M)
Benjamin Tubbs (M)
Abraham Yarrington (M)

Capt. Fitch Bissell's company
John Atwood (M)
Orias Atwood (M)
Elisha Boardman (M)
Samuel Boardman (M)
Ira Clark (M)
Roderick Clark (M)
William Craddock (M)
John Fletcher (M)
Abner Fuller (M)
Lemuel Fuller (M)
Jonathan Halladay (M)
Hezekiah Haydon (M)
Carmi Higley (M)
Eleazer House (M)
Erastus Humphrey (M)
Robert Newcomb (M)
Aaron Porter (M)
Cornelius Russel (M)
Roger Tyler (M)
John Wilson (M)
John White (M)

Capt. Hubbard's company
Eleazer Brooks (M)
Samuel Buck Jr. (M)
Ebenezer Coe (M)
Cornelius Coverling (M)
Aaron Drake (M)
Benjamin Hills (M)
Alexander Ingham (M)
Elias Leet (M)
Levi Loveland (M)
William Parsons (M)
Elijah Roberts (M)
Reuben Shipman (M)
Samuel Skinner (M)
Samuel Strictland (M)
William Talmage (M)
Seth Turner (M)
Job Wetmore (M)
Nathan Whiting (M)

BIBLIOGRAPHY

BOOKS

Allen, W.B., ed. *George Washington, A Collection.* Indianapolis, IN: Liberty Fund, 1988.

Anderson, Fred. *A People's Army: Massachusetts Soldiers and Society in the Seven Years' War.* Chapel Hill: University of North Carolina Press, 1984.

———. *Crucible of War: The Seven Years' War and the Fate of Empire in British North America.* New York: Vintage Books, 2000.

Bliven, Bruce Jr. *Under the Guns: New York: 1775–1776.* New York: Harper and Row, 1972.

Brainerd, M. *Life of Rev. Thomas Brainerd, D.D.* Philadelphia: J. B. Lippincott & Co., 1870.

Brumwell, Stephen. *White Devil: A True Story of War, Savagery, and Vengeance in Colonial America.* New York: Da Capo Press, 2005.

Chartrand, René. *Ticonderoga 1758: Montcalm's Victory Against All Odds.* Oxford: Osprey Publishing, 2000.

Clark, Delphina L.H. *Phineas Lyman, Connecticut's General.* Springfield, MA: Connecticut Valley Historical Museum, 1964.

Cummings, Abbott Lowell, ed. *Rural Household Inventories: Establishing the Names, Uses and Furnishings of Rooms in the Colonial New England Home, 1675–1775.* Boston: The Society for the Preservation of New England Antiquities, 1964.

Drake, Francis S. *The Town of Roxbury.* Roxbury, MA: published by the author, 1878. Facsimile reprint, Westminster, MD: Heritage Books, 1994.

Dusen, Albert E. *Connecticut.* New York: Random House, 1961.

Edgar, Gregory T. *Reluctant Break with Britain: From Stamp Act to Bunker Hill.* Bowie, MD: Heritage Books, 1997.

Forbes, Esther. *Paul Revere and the World He Lived In.* Boston: Houghton Mifflin Company, 1942.

Gallagher, John J. *The Battle of Brooklyn 1776.* Edison, NJ: Castle Books, 1995.

Galvin, John R. *The Minute Men, The First Fight: Myths and Realities of the American Revolution.* Washington, D.C.: Potomac Books, Inc., 2006.

Gardiner, Robert, ed., *The Line of Battle: The Sailing Warship 1650–1840.* London: Conway Maritime Press, 1992.

Guinness, Alison C. "The Life and Times of General Joseph Spencer of East Haddam, Connecticut, 1714–1789." University of Connecticut, 1997.

Guthman, William H. *Drums A'Beating, Trumpets Sounding: Artistically Carved Powder Horns in the Provincial Manner 1746–1781*. Hartford: Connecticut Historical Society, 1993.

Humphreys, David. *An Essay on the Life of the Honorable Major-General Israel Putnam*. Indianapolis, IN: Liberty Fund, 2000.

Hyneman, Charles S., and Donald S. Lutz. *American Political Writing During the Founding Era, 1760–1805*. Indianapolis, IN: Liberty Fund, 2000.

Johnson, Michael. *Tribes of the Iroquois Confederacy*. Oxford, UK: Osprey Publishing, 2003.

———. *American Woodland Indians*. Oxford, UK: Osprey/Reed International Books, 1990.

Johnston, Henry P., ed. *The Record of Connecticut Men in the Military and Naval Service During the War of the Revolution, 1775–1783*. Hartford, CT: Press of the Case, Lockwood, and Brainard Co., 1889.

———. *The Campaign of 1776 Around New York and Brooklyn*. Cranbury, NJ: The Scholars Bookshelf, 2005.

Katcher, Philip. *Uniforms of the Continental Army*. York, PA: George Shumway Publisher, 1981.

Kemmer, Brenton C. *Redcoats, Yankees and Allies*. Westminster, MD: Heritage Books, 2007.

Ketchum, Richard M. *Decisive Day: The Battle for Bunker Hill*. New York: Henry Holt and Co., 1999.

Leach, Douglas Edward. *Roots of Conflict: British Armed Forces and Colonial Americans, 1677–1763*. Chapel Hill: University of North Carolina Press, 1986.

Leckie, Robert. *A Few Acres of Snow: The Saga of the French and Indian Wars*. New York: John Wiley & Sons, 1999.

Lucier, Armand Francis. *French and Indian War Notices Abstracted From Colonial Newspapers*. 4 vols. Bowie, MD: Heritage Books, 1999.

———. *Newspaper Datelines of the American Revolution*. 4 vols. Bowie, MD: Heritage Books, 1999.

Malcomson, Robert. *Warships of the Great Lakes, 1754–1834*. Edison, NJ: Knickerbocker Press, 2004.

May, Robin. *Wolfe's Army*. Men-At-Arms series 48. London: Osprey Military, 1996.

McCulloch, Ian Macpherson. *Sons of the Mountain: The Highland Regiments in the French and Indian War, 1756–1767*. New York: Purple Mountain Press, 2006.

McCullough, David. *1776*. New York: Simon and Schuster Paperbacks, 2005.

Morgan, Edward S. and Helen M. *The Stamp Act Crisis*. New York: Collier Books, 1976.

Morrissey, Brendan. *Boston 1775: The Shot Heard Around the World.* Oxford: Osprey Publishing, 1995.

_____. *Saratoga 1777: Turning Point of a Revolution.* Oxford: Osprey Publishing, 2000.

Niles, Hosford B. *The Old Chimney Stacks of East Haddam.* New York: Lowe & Co., 1887.

Parker, Francis H. *Contributions to the History of East Haddam, Ct.* Hartford: Connecticut State Library, 1938.

Parkman, Francis. *Montcalm and Wolfe.* New York: Barnes and Noble Books, 2005.

Philbrick, Nathaniel. *Mayflower.* New York: Penguin Books, 2006.

Price, Carl F. *Yankee Township.* East Hampton, CT: Citizen's Welfare Club, 1941.

_____. *Postscripts to Yankee Township.* East Hampton, CT: East Hampton Bicentennial Committee, 1975.

Roberts, George S. *Historic Towns of the Connecticut River Valley.* Schenectady, NY: Robson and Adee Publishers, c1906. Digitized and published online, Hamden, CT: the Arnold Bernhard Library, Quinnipiac University, March 2005.

Royster, Charles. *A Revolutionary People at War.* Chapel Hill: University of North Carolina Press, 1979.

Sandoz, Ellis, ed. *Political Sermons of the American Founding Era.* Vol. 1 (1730–1788). 2nd ed. Indianapolis, IN: Liberty Fund, 1998.

Schechter, Barnet. *The Battle for New York.* New York: Walker & Co., 2002.

Selesky, Harold E. *War & Society in Colonial Connecticut.* New Haven, CT: Yale University Press, 1990.

Steele, Ian K. *Betrayals: Fort William Henry & the "Massacre."* New York: Oxford University Press, 1990.

Urban, Mark. *Fusiliers: The Saga of a British Redcoat Regiment in the American Revolution.* New York: Walker & Company, 2007.

Van Dusen, Albert E. *Connecticut.* New York: Random House, 1961.

Williams, Noel St. John. *Redcoats Along the Hudson.* London: Brasseys, 1997.

REFERENCE WORKS

Fuller, William Hyslop. *Genealogy of Some of the Descendants of Edward Fuller of the Mayflower.* Palmer, MA: C.B. Fiske & Co., 1908.

History of Dearborn and Ohio Counties, Indiana. Chicago: F.E. Weakley & Co., 1885.

Hoadley, Charles J., ed. *The Public Records of the Colony of Connecticut, From May, 1751, to February, 1757 Inclusive.* Hartford, CT: Press of the Case, Lockwood, and Brainard Co., 1877.

———. *The Public Records of the Colony of Connecticut, From May, 1757, to March, 1776 Inclusive*. Hartford, CT: Press of the Case, Lockwood, and Brainard Co., 1880.

———. *The Public Records of the Colony of Connecticut*. Vol. 13, *May 1769*. Hartford, CT: Press of the Case, Lockwood, and Brainard Co, 1885.

———. *The Public Records of the State of Connecticut, From May, 1778, to April, 1780 Inclusive*. Vol. 2. Hartford, CT: Press of the Case, Lockwood, and Brainard Co., 1880.

Rolls of Connecticut Men in the French and Indian War, 1755–1762. *Collections of the Connecticut Historical Society*, vols. 9, 10. Hartford: published by the society, 1903, 1905.

DIARIES, JOURNALS, MEMOIRS AND OTHER PRIMARY SOURCES

"An Orderly Book From April 1775 to September 1775 During the Siege of Boston." *Proceedings of the Massachusetts Historical Society*, vol. 15. Boston: published by the society, 1876–1877.

Arnot, Hugh. "Extract of the Journal of Hugh Arnot." *Bulletin of the Fort Ticonderoga Museum* 16, no. 1 (1998): 22–43.

Bangs, Isaac. *Journal of Lieutenant Isaac Bangs, April 1 to July 29, 1776*. Edward Bangs, ed. Eyewitness Accounts of the American Revolution series. New York: New York Times and Arno Press, 1968.

Bixby, Samuel. "Diary of Samuel Bixby." *Proceedings of the Massachusetts Historical Society*, vol. 14. Boston: published by the society, 1876–1877: 285–298.

———. "Letters Illustrating the Siege." *Proceedings of the Massachusetts Historical Society*, vol. 14. Boston: published by the society, 1876–1877: 275–285.

Blodget, Samuel. "A Prospective Plan of the Battle Near Lake George, on the Eighth Day of September, 1755." Boston, 1755.

Bonin, Jolicoeur Charles. *Memoir of a French and Indian War Soldier*. Andrew Gallup, ed. Westminster, MD: Heritage Books, 1993.

Booth, Joseph. "Journal Kept by Joseph Booth, 1760." French and Indian War Papers, Connecticut Historical Society, Hartford.

Bougainville, Louis Antoine de, and Edward Pierce Hamilton. *Adventure in the Wilderness: the American Journals of Louis Antoine de Bougainville, 1756–1760*. Translated and edited by Edward P. Hamilton. Norman: University of Oklahoma Press, 1964.

Brainard, Homer W. *James Percival of Sandwich, Massachusetts and Some of His Descendants*. Hartford, CT: printed by author, 1925.

Claus, Daniel. "Daniel Claus' Narrative of His Relations with Sir William Johnson and Experiences in the Lake George Fight." New York: Society of Colonial Wars in the State of New York, 1904.

Comstock, Christopher. "Journal of Christopher Comstock of Chatham, Connecticut, Kept While Serving in the French and Indian War, 1758–1759." Connecticut Historical Society, Hartford.

Connecticut Archives: Revolutionary War, series 1, 5.

Connecticut Archives: Revolutionary War, series 1, 12.

"Correspondence of the Brothers Joshua and Jedediah Huntington during the Period of the American Revolution." In Huntington Papers, *Collections of the Connecticut Historical Society*, vol. 20. Hartford: published by the society, 1923.

Dimmick, Ryan. *Descendants of Thomas Dymoke: The Dimmick Family Tree*, http://www.dimmicks.com/generation4.htm. Accessed January 7, 2010.

Dwight, Melatiah Everett. "The Journal of Captain Nathaniel Dwight of Belchertown, Mass., During the Crown Point Expedition 1755." *The New York Genealogical and Biographical Record* 33 (January and April 1902): 3–10; 65–70, 164–166.

Emerson, William. *Diaries and Letters of William Emerson, 1743–1776*. Amelia Forbes Emerson, ed. Boston: Thomas Todd, 1972.

Estabrook, Hobart. *The Praying Warrior, Mr. Estabrook's Sermon, Preached May 30, 1758*. New Haven: James Parker & Co., 1758.

Fitch, Jabez, Jr. *The Diary of Jabez Fitch, Jr. in the French and Indian War, 1757*. Third edition. New York State French & Indian War 250th Anniversary Commemoration Commission and Rogers Island Heritage Development Alliance, 2007.

———. "A Journal, from August 5th to December 13th, 1775. Kept by Lieutenant Jabez Fitch, Jr., of Norwich, of the 8th Company, Capt. Joseph Jewett's, in the Eighth Connecticut Regiment, Col. Jedidiah Huntington's, at the siege of Boston." In *Proceedings of the Massachusetts Historical Society*, series 2, vol. 9, 41–91. Boston: published by the society, 1894–1895.

———. *The New-York Diary of Lieutenant Jabez Fitch of the 17th (Connecticut) Regiment From August 22, 1776 to December 15, 1777*. W.H. W. Sabine, ed. New York: Colburn & Tegg, 1954.

———. Jabez Fitch Diary, January 4, 1776 to April 6, 1776. Transcribed by Carol and George Gadbois. Peter Force Collection, Manuscript Division, Library of Congress.

———. *The Diary of Jabez Fitch, a Prison-Ship Martyr of 1776*. New York: William Abbatt, 1903.

Hawks, John. *Orderly Book and Journal of Major John Hawks, on the Ticonderoga-Crown Point Campaign, Under General Jeffrey Amherst 1759–1760*. Society of Colonial Wars in the State of New York. New York: H.K. Brewer & Co., 1911.

Hill, James. "The Diary of A Private on the First Expedition to Crown Point, Diary of James Hill." Edna V. Moffett, ed. *The New England Quarterly* 5 (July 1932): 602–618.

Knox, John, and Arthur G. Doughty. *An Historical Journal of the Campaigns in North America for the Years 1757, 1758, 1759, and 1760.* Vol I–III. Toronto: Champlain Society, 1914.

Letter from Major Joseph Spencer, June 6, 1758. French and Indian War Papers, box 2, file 16, Connecticut Historical Society, Hartford.

MacGunnigle, Bruce Campbell. *Mayflower Families Through Five Generations—Descendants of the Pilgrims Who Landed at Plymouth, Mass. Dec 1620.* Vol. 4: Edward Fuller. Plymouth, MA: General Society of Mayflower Descendants, 1990.

Mack, Solomon. *A Narraitve* [sic] *of the Life of Solomon Mack.* Windsor: self-printed, 1811.

Martin, Joseph Plumb. *Private Yankee Doodle.* George E. Scheer, ed. New York: Eastern Acorn Press, 1988.

Orderly Book of Colonel Nathan Whiting. Microfilm collection, Connecticut State Library, Hartford. L.H. 4393/94.

Perry, David. "Recollections of an Old Soldier . . . Written by Himself." *Magazine of History* 137 (1928). Reprinted from a pamphlet by the same title, Windsor, VT, 1822.

Peters, Nathan and Lois. *The Correspondence of Captain and Lois Peters.* William H. Guthman, ed. Hartford: Connecticut Historical Society, 1980.

Pouchot, Pierre. *Memoirs on the Late War in North America Between France and England.* Brian Leigh Dunnigan, ed., Michael Cardy, trans. New York: Old Fort Niagara Publishing, 1994.

Rea, Caleb. "The Journal of Caleb Rea, Written During the Expedition Against Ticonderoga in 1758, edited by his great grandson F.M. Ray." *Essex Institute Historical Collections* 18, nos. 1, 2, 3. Salem, MA: Salem Press, 1881.

Rogers, Robert. "Reminiscences of the French War; Containing Rogers' Expeditions." 1831. In *Reminiscences of the French War,* 1–191. Freedom, NH: Freedom Historical Society, 1988.

Sullivan, Thomas. *From Redcoat to Rebel, The Thomas Sullivan Journal.* Joseph Lee Boyle, ed. Westminster, MD: Heritage Books, 1997.

Thacher, James. *Military Journal of the American Revolution 1775–1783.* Gansevoort: Corner House Historical Publications, 1998.

Tomlinson, Abraham, ed. *Military Journals of Two Private Soldiers, 1758–1775. Supplement Containing Official Papers on the Skirmishes at Lexington and Concord.* Poughkeepsie, NY: Tomlinson, 1855.

Trowbridge, Francis Bacon, ed. *The Champion Genealogy: A History of the Descendants of Henry Champion.* New Haven: printed for the author, 1891.

"Verses Relating to the Events of 1755." *Proceedings of the Massachusetts Historical Society,* series 2, vol. 9. Boston: published by the society, 1894–1895. 2–5.

Warner, Jennifer S. *Boone County: From Mastodons to the Millennium.* Boone County, KY: Bicentennial Book Committee, 1998.

Waterman, Asa. *Asa Waterman's Diary*. Worcester, MA: American Antiquarian Society. No known publisher.

Webb, Samuel Blachley. *Correspondence and Journals of Samuel Blachley Webb*. Worthington Chauncey Ford, ed. New York and Lancaster, PA: Wickersham Press, 1893. Reprinted by New York: Arno Press, 1969.

Webster, J. Clarence, ed. *The Journal of Jeffrey Amherst: Recording the Military Career of General Amherst in America from 1758 to 1763*. Toronto and Chicago: Ryerson Press and University of Chicago Press, 1931.

Wells, Edmund. *Diary of Edmund Wells—Captain from Hebron, Connecticut*. Hartford: Connecticut Historical Society, 1923. June 14 – November 20, 1756.

Whiting, Nathan. "Letters of Colonel Nathan Whiting, Written From Camp During the French and Indian War." Lemuel A. Welles, ed. *Papers of the New Haven Colony Historical Society*. Vol. 11. New Haven, 1900.

Colonel Whiting's Regimental Daily Roll of August 14, 1758. French and Indian War Papers, box 1, folder 9, Connecticut Historical Society, Hartford, CT.

Whittemore, Henry J. *History of Middlesex County, Connecticut, with Special Sketches of its Prominent Men*. New York: J. B. Beers & Co., 1884.

ARTICLES

Cardwell, M. John. "Mismanagement: The 1758 Expedition Against Carillon." *Bulletin of the Fort Ticonderoga Museum* 15, no. 4 (1992).

Connecticut Courant, April 22, 1776.

Connecticut Society of the Sons of the American Revolution. "The Scarlet Standard No. 2," August 1997. http://www.connecticutsar.org/articles/scarlet_no2.htm.

Davies, Stephen. "Estimated Population of American Colonies: 1610 to 1780." http://web.viu.ca/davies/H320/population.colonies.htm. Accessed February 23, 2010.

Hartley, L. "Mary Fuller Percival, a Humanitarian." *National Historical Magazine*, May 1941.

New Hampshire Gazette, September 8, 1758. Online at *Archiving Early America*. http://www.earlyamerica.com/review/1998/scalpins.html.

U.S. Census Bureau. Connecticut, Delaware, Massachusetts, Kentucky, Indiana Territory for 1800 and 1820. http://www2.census.gov/prod2/decennial/documents/1820a-02.pdf. Accessed April 9, 2010.

Wikipedia. "Smallpox," http://wikipedia.org/wiki/smallpox; and "Population history of indigenous peoples of the Americas," http://wikipedia.org/wiki/population_history_of_american_indigenous_peoples. Accessed January 17, 2010.

DANIEL D. KINLEY

PUBLIC RECORDS

Boone County, KY, deed records
Boone County, Kentucky County, KY, court orders 1799–1815
Boone County, KY, tax records
Land records, Chatham (East Hampton), CT
Land records, East Haddam, CT
Probate records, East Haddam, CT
1790 census, Freehold, Albany County, NY
1790 census, Marlborough, Middlesex County, MA
1800 census, Freehold, Albany County, NY
1810 census, Boone County, KY
1810 census, Durham, Greene County, NY
Public land records of East Hampton and East Haddam, vol. 3, pages 1–5, March 10, 1774.

MISCELLANEOUS PAMPHLETS

Brainard, Homer W. "Henry Rowley and Some of His Descendants." *New York Genealogical and Biographical Record* 37 (1906). 98–99.
Committee on Historical Documents and Lake George Memorial Committee of the Society of Colonial Wars in the State of New York, comp. *Battle of Lake George, September 8, 1755*. April 1897. Reprint, n.p.: Buckle Press, 1991.
New York State Museum. "A Mohawk Iroquois Village." http://www.nysm.nysed.gov/IroquoisVillage/constructiontwo.html. Accessed January 2010.
"Weather—1758 Campaign." Fort Ticonderoga Association Research File. July 24, 1995.

ENDNOTES

CHAPTER 1

1. Homer W. Brainard, *James Percival of Sandwich and Some of His Descendants* (Hartford: n.p., 1925), 18.
2. Ibid., 20B.
3. Francis Parkman, *Montcalm and Wolfe* (New York: Barnes and Noble Books, 2005), 12–14.
4. Louise Hartley, "Mary Fuller Percival, a Humanitarian," *National Historical Magazine*, May 1941, 26–27.
5. Brainard, 19.
6. Ibid., 18–19.
7. M. Brainerd, *Life of Rev. Thomas Brainerd, D.D.* (Philadelphia: J. B. Lippincott & Co., 1870), 13.
8. Charles J. Hoadley, ed., *The Public Records of the Colony of Connecticut, From May, 1751, to February, 1757, Inclusive* (Hartford, CT: Press of the Case, Lockwood, and Brainard Co., 1877), 394.
9. *Descendants of Thomas Dymoke: The Dimmick Family Tree*, http://www.dimmicks.com/ generation4.htm. Accessed January 7, 2010.
10. Rolls of Connecticut Men in the French and Indian War, 1755–1762, in *Collections of the Connecticut Historical Society*, vol. 9 (Hartford: by the society, 1905), 73.
11. Hoadley, 349.
12. Abbott Lowell Cummings, ed. *Rural Household Inventories: Establishing the Names, Uses and Furnishings of Rooms in the Colonial New England Home, 1675–1775* (Boston: Society for the Preservation of New England Antiquities, 1964). I've extrapolated the cost of a cow based on various inventories, 150–241.
13. Rolls of Connecticut Men in the French and Indian War, 1755–1762, vol. 9, 73.
14. Parkman, 156.
15. Ibid., 158.
16. Ibid., 157.
17. As a Revolutionary War re-enactor, I have had to endure, like Timothy, holding a 15-pound musket straight out in front of me while the commander inspects the entire line of our troops. It does take only a few

moments before the strain of the weight on the unaccustomed arm positions begins to take its toll; we remember to ensure that our weapons are in good order for the next drill so to speed the commander on to the completion of his inspection.

18. Armand Francis Lucier, *French and Indian War Notices Abstracted From Colonial Newspapers*, vol. 1. (Bowie, MD: Heritage Books, 1999), 280.
19. Parkman, 93.
20. Louis Antoine de Bougainville and Edward Pierce Hamilton, *Adventure in the Wilderness; the American Journals of Louis Antoine de Bougainville, 1756–1760*, Edward P. Hamilton, ed. and trans. (Norman: University of Oklahoma Press, 1964), 118.
21. Parkman, 161–162.
22. Committee on Historical Documents and Lake George Memorial Committee of the Society of Colonial Wars in the State of New York, comp., *Battle of Lake George, September 8, 1755* (reprint, Buckle Press, 1991; first published April 1897), 3.
23. Ibid., 3–4.
24. Samuel Blodget, "A Prospective Plan of the Battle Near Lake George, on the Eighth Day of September, 1755," Boston, MA, 1755, 2.
25. Committee on Historical Documents, *Battle of Lake* George, 12.
26. Lucier, vol. 1, 319–320.
27. Melatiah Everett Dwight, "The Journal of Captain Nathaniel Dwight of Belchertown, Mass., During the Crown Point Expedition 1755." *New York Genealogical and Biographical Record* 33 (January 1902), 7–9.
28. Ibid., 68.
29. Rolls of Connecticut Men in the French and Indian War, 1755–1762, in *Collections of the Connecticut Historical Society*, vol. 9 (Hartford: published by the society, 1905), 74–75.
30. Brainard, 19, 26.
31. "Verses Relating to the Events of 1755," in *Proceedings of the Massachusetts Historical Society*, series 2, vol. 9 [vol. 29 of continuous numbering] (Boston: published by the society, 1894–1895), 3.

CHAPTER 2

32. Armand Francis Lucier, *French and Indian War Notices Abstracted From Colonial Newspapers*, vol. I, November, December, 1755; vol. 2, January, February, March, 1756 (Bowie, MD: Heritage Books, Inc., 1999). Newspapers published in Philadelphia, Elizabeth-Town and New York report on Indian attacks along frontier communities in Virginia, Delaware, Maryland, eastern Pennsylvania, and New York. A dispatch from the *Pennsylvania Gazette* in Philadelphia reads: "The barbarous and bloody Scene which is now opened in the Upper Parts of Northampton County, is the most lamentable that perhaps ever appeared; —There is no Person who is possessed of any Humanity, but would commiserate the deplorable Fate of these unhappy People: There may be seen Horror and Desolation; — populous settlements deserted; — Villages laid to Ashes; — Men, Women and Children cruelly mangled and massacred; — some found

in the Woods, every nauscous for want of Interment: Some just reeking from the Hands of their Savage Slaughterers some hacked and covered all over with Wounds."
33. Nathaniel Philbrick, *Mayflower* (New York: Viking, 2006), 299.
34. Bruce Campbell MacGunnigle, comp., David L. Greene, ed., *Mayflower Families Through Five Generations—Descendants of the Pilgrims Who Landed at Plymouth, Mass. Dec 1620*, vol. 4: Edward Fuller family (Plymouth: General Society of Mayflower Descendants, 1990), 8–9.
35. Charles J. Hoadley, ed., *The Public Records of the Colony of Connecticut, From May, 1751, to February, 1757, Inclusive* (Hartford: Case, Lockwood & Brainard Co., 1877), 475.
36. Rolls of Connecticut Men in the French and Indian Wars, 1755–1762, in *Collections of the Connecticut Historical Society*, vol. 9 (Hartford: Connecticut Historical Society, 1903), 148.
37. Hoadley, 475.
38. Edmund Wells, *Diary of Edmund Wells—Captain from Hebron, Connecticut* (Hartford: Connecticut Historical Society), preface.
39. William Hyslop Fuller, *Genealogy of Some of the Descendants of Edward Fuller of the Mayflower* (Palmer: C.B. Fiske & Co., 1908), 149.
40. Jabez Fitch Jr., *The Diary of Jabez Fitch, Jr. in the French and Indian War, 1757*, 3rd ed. (New York State French & Indian War 250th Anniversary Commemoration Commission and Rogers Island Heritage Development Alliance, 2007), 12.
41. Michael G. Johnson, *American Woodland Indians* (England: Osprey/Reed International, 1990), 21.
42. Wells, 2, 3.
43. Stephen Brumwell, *White Devil* (Great Britain: Weidenfeld & Nicolson, 2004), 101–103; also Robin May, *Wolfe's Army*, Men-At-Arms series 48 (London: Osprey Military, 1996), 28.
44. Wells, 3–5.
45. I use the language of the time to refer to British soldiers as "regulars," and soldiers raised by and fighting for individual colonies as "provincials" or "colonials."
46. Wells, 3.
47. Robin May, *Wolfe's Army*, Men-At-Arms series 48 (London: Osprey Military, 1996), 27, 43.
48. Fred Anderson, *Crucible of War* (New York: Vintage Books, 2000), 139–146.
49. Wells, 5–7.
50. Ibid., 10–11.
51. Ibid., 11.
52. Ibid., 12.
53. Louis Antoine de Bougainville, *Adventures in the Wilderness: the American Journals of Antoine de Bougainville 1756–1760*, Edward P. Hamilton, ed. and trans. (Norman: University of Oklahoma Press, 1964), 49.
54. Wells, 12, 13.
55. Ibid., 13.
56. Ibid., 13–22.

57. Rolls of Connecticut Men in the French and Indian Wars, vol. 9, 148.
58. Ibid., 187–188. The muster list shows the name: Joel Negro.
59. Ibid., 202–203.
60. Ian K. Steele, *Betrayals: Fort William Henry & the "Massacre"* (New York: Oxford University Press, 1990), 125.
61. Homer W. Brainard, *Henry Rowley and Some of His Descendants* (Hartford, CT, 1906), 98–99.

CHAPTER 3

62. Fred Anderson, *Crucible of War* (New York: Vintage Books, 2000), 210.
63. Rolls of Connecticut Men in the French and Indian War, 1755–1762, in *Collections of the Connecticut Historical Society*, vol. 10 (Hartford: published by the society, 1905), 34, 35.
64. Charles J. Hoadley, ed. *The Public Records of the Colony of Connecticut, From May, 1757, to March, 1762 Inclusive* (Hartford: Press of the Case, Lockwood, and Brainard Co., 1880), 99.
65. Ibid., 94.
66. Rolls of Connecticut Men, vol. 10, 35.
67. Ibid., 34–36.
68. Alison C. Guinness, *The Life and Times of General Joseph Spencer of East Haddam, Connecticut, 1714–1789*, 3–4.
69. Hobart Estabrook, *The Praying Warrior, Mr. Estabrook's Sermon, Preached May 30, 1758* (New Haven: James Parker & Co., 1758).
70. Letter from Major Joseph Spencer, June 6, 1758, French and Indian War Papers, box 2, file 16, Connecticut Historical Society, Hartford.
71. Rolls of Connecticut Men, vol. 10, 36.
72. "Orderly Book of Colonel Nathan Whiting," Connecticut State Library Microfilm Collection, L.H. 4393/94, Hartford, Connecticut, June 15, 1758, entry.
73. M. John Cardwell, "Mismanagement: The 1758 Expedition Against Carillon," *Bulletin of the Fort Ticonderoga Museum* 15, no. 4 (1992), 265–266.
74. Ibid., 255–256.
75. Weather—1758 Campaign. A Fort Ticonderoga Research File. July 24, 1995. Throughout this chapter, references to the weather are taken from this document.
76. Cardwell, 252.
77. René Chartrand, *Ticonderoga 1758, Montcalm's Victory Against All Odds* (Oxford: Osprey Publishing, 2000), 26–29.
78. Louis-Antoine de Bougainville, *Adventure in the Wilderness: the American Journals of Louis Antoine de Bougainville, 1756–1760*. De Bougainville notes in entries for November 8, 1757 (page 192), "The smallpox made great ravages this year. Generally, it comes only every twenty years; however it has now reigned for two," and December (page 193), "The smallpox has made great ravages again among the Indians of the Far West." In an April 12, 1758, entry, he says "First, I note that all winter only part of the Indians have come, proof of their coolness, since last year they were here all the time." And in a May 1758 entry (page 204) he says, "The Ottawas

have evil designs. The Potawatomis indisposed. Finally, [the relations of] all these relations [with us] are on the decline. What is the cause of it? The great loss they have suffered from the smallpox, the bad medicine the French have thrown to them, the great greed of the commanders of the posts and their ignorance of Indian customs?"
79. Armand Francis Lucier, *French and Indian War Notices Abstracted From Colonial Newspapers*, vol. 3 (Bowie, MD: Heritage Books, 1999), 93.
80. "Orderly Book of Colonel Nathan Whiting," June 28, 1758, entry.
81. "Orderly Book of Colonel Nathan Whiting," July 1, 1758, entry.
82. Lucier, 101.
83. Ian Macpherson McCulloch, *Sons of the Mountains: The Highland Regiments in the French and Indian War, 1756–1767* (New York: Purple Mountain Press, 2006), 85.
84. Francis Parkman, *Montcalm and Wolfe* (New York: Barnes and Noble Books, 2005), 329.
85. Anderson, 241–242.
86. Parkman, 330.
87. Hugh Arnot, "Extract of the Journal of Hugh Arnot," *Bulletin of the Fort Ticonderoga Museum* 16, no. 1 (1998), 35–36.
88. Parkman, 330.
89. Ibid., 330–332.
90. Ibid., 331–332.
91. Bougainville, 230.
92. Parkman, 333.
93. Chartrand, 45.
94. McCulloch, 93.
95. Parkman, 334–335.
96. Chartrand, 61–62.
97. Parkman, 335.
98. Chartrand, 64–65.
99. Parkman, 336.
100. Chartrand, 64.
101. Chartrand, 55–56.
102. David Perry, "Recollections of an Old Soldier . . . Written by Himself," *Magazine of History* 137 (1928), 9–10. Reprinted from a pamphlet by the same title, Windsor, VT, 1822.
103. McCulloch, 101–102.
104. Ibid., 104–105.
105. Francis Bacon Trowbridge, *The Champion Genealogy: A History of the Descendants of Henry Champion*, (New Haven, 1891), 419.
106. Ibid., 419.
107. "Orderly Book of Colonel Nathan Whiting," July 11, 1758, entry.
108. Trowbridge, 419–420.
109. Caleb Rea. "The Journal of Caleb Rea, written during the expedition against Ticonderoga in 1758, edited by his great grandson F.M. Ray." Essex Institute Historical Collections XVIII, no. 1, 2, 3. (Salem: The Salem Press, 1881), 107.
110. Ibid., 111.

111. Anderson, 247–248.
112. Parkman, 340–341.
113. Rolls of Connecticut Men, vol. 10, 36.
114. Robert Rogers, "Reminiscences of the French War; Containing Rogers' Expeditions" (1831), in *Reminiscences of the French War* (Freedom: Freedom Historical Society, 1988), 71–72.
115. Solomon Mack, *A Narraitve* [sic] *of the Life of Solomon Mack* (Windsor: Self-Printed, 1811), 8–9.
116. David Humphreys, *An Essay on the Life of the Honorable Major-General Israel Putnam* (Indianapolis, Liberty Fund, 2000), 43.
117. This is based on my experience as a historical re-enactor.
118. Mack, 8.
119. New Hampshire Gazette, September 8, 1758, www.earlyamerica.com/review/1998/scalping.html. Solomon Mack also notes that "Ensign Worcester had nine wounds, scalped and tomahawked, who lived and got well." *A Narraitve* [sic] *of the Life of Solomon Mack*, 8.
120. Mack, 9.
121. Rolls of Connecticut Men, vol. 10, 35.
122. "Orderly Book of Colonel Nathan Whiting," August 12, 1758, entry.
123. Ibid., August 13, 1758, entry.
124. Colonel Whiting's Regimental Daily Roll of August 14, 1758, French and Indian War Papers, box 1, folder 9, Connecticut Historical Society, Hartford, CT. Lists Ensign Percival and Major Spencer on duty with General Lyman.
125. "Orderly Book of Colonel Nathan Whiting," August 13, 1758, entry.
126. Trowbridge, 426.
127. "Orderly Book of Colonel Nathan Whiting," September 29, 1758, entry.
128. Anderson, 287.
129. Rolls of Connecticut Men, vol. 10, 35–36.
130. Trowbridge, 432–434.
131. Ibid., 433.
132. Ibid., 434.
133. Ibid., 434.
134. Ibid., 434–435.
135. Rolls of Connecticut Men, vol. 10, 35.

CHAPTER 4

136. Charles J. Hoadly, ed. *The Public Records of the Colony of Connecticut, from May, 1757, to March, 1762 Inclusive*. (Hartford: Press of the Case, Lockwood, and Brainard Co., 1880), 222–225.
137. Ibid., 226.
138. Rolls of Connecticut Men in the French and Indian War, 1755–1762, in *Collections of the Connecticut Historical Society*, vol. 10 (Hartford:by the society, 1905), 127–128.
139. Ibid. This figure was arrived at by checking the men's names in the indexes of Rolls of Connecticut Men in the French and Indian War, 1755–1762, vols. 9 and 10.

140. Hoadley, 351–352.
141. Harold E. Selesky, *War & Society in Colonial Connecticut*, (New Haven: Yale University Press, 1990), 140.
142. Hoadley, 387.
143. Abbott Lowell Cummings, ed., *Rural Household Inventories: Establishing the Names, Uses and Furnishings of Rooms in the Colonial New England Home, 1675–1775* (Boston: The Society for the Preservation of New England Antiquities, 1964). I've estimated the price of hogs in 1760 by extrapolating costs from assorted final inventories, 150–241.
144. Rolls of Connecticut Men in the French and Indian War, 1755–1762, vol. 10, 194.
145. Ibid., 196.
146. Selesky, 168, table 5.4.
147. Rolls of Connecticut Men in the French and Indian War, 1755–1762, vol. 10, 192.
148. Ibid., 195–196.
149. Joseph Booth, "Journal Kept by Joseph Booth, 1760," French and Indian War Papers Collection, Connecticut Historical Society, Hartford; June 17, 1760, entry.
150. Delphina L.H. Clark, *Phineas Lyman, Connecticut's General* (Springfield: Connecticut Valley Historical Museum, 1964), 50.
151. Wikipedia entries on smallpox and indigenous populations, http://wikipedia.org/wiki/smallpox, and http://wikipedia.org/wiki/population_history_of_american_indigenous_peoples, Accessed January 17, 2010.
152. Clark, 50.
153. Booth, June 19, 1760, entry.
154. J. Clarence Webster, ed., *The Journal of Jeffrey Amherst: Recording the Military Career of General Amherst in America from 1758 to 1763* (Toronto and Chicago: The Ryerson Press/University of Chicago Press, 1931), 212.
155. Ibid., 212–213.
156. New York State Museum, http://www.nysed.gov.IroquoisVillage/constructiontwo.html.
157. Webster, June 10, 1760; entry, 209; and June 19, 1760, entry, 212.
158. Ibid., June 30, 1760, entry, 215.
159. Ibid., July 6, 1760, entry, 216.
160. Ibid., July 9, 1760, entry, 217.
161. Ibid., July 23, 1760, entry, 221.
162. Ibid., July 24, 1760, entry, 221.
163. Ibid., July 28, 1760, entry, 222.
164. Robert Gardiner, ed., *The Line of Battle* (London: Conway Maritime Press, 1992), 129.
165. Robert Malcomson, *Warships of the Great Lakes, 1754–1834* (Edison, NJ: Knickerbocker Press, 2004), 18.
166. Ibid., 17.
167. Webster, 217–222. From July 9 through 27, Amherst reports sightings of enemy vessels and subsequently urging Loring to sail against the enemy ships. When Loring returns, Amherst does not mention Loring's having successfully engaged the French.

DANIEL D. KINLEY

168. Ibid., July 29, 1760, entry, 222.
169. John Knox, *Historical Journal of the Campaigns in North America* (Toronto: Champlain Society, 1916), 527–528.
170. Brenton C. Kemmer, *Redcoats, Yankees and Allies* (Westminster, MD: Heritage Books, 2007), 108.
171. Knox, 540.
172. Webster, July 30, 1760, entry, 222–223.
173. Ibid., August 1, 3, 1760, entries, 223–224.
174. Ibid., August 5, 1760, entry, 224–225.
175. Ibid., August 6, 8, 9, 1760, entries, 225–226.
176. Ibid., August 11, 1760, entry, 228.
177. Ibid., August 11, 1760, entry, 228.
178. Ibid., August 13, 14, 15, 1760, entries, 229–231.
179. Ibid., August 17, 18, 1760, entries, 231–232.
180. Pierre Pouchot, *Memoirs on the Late War in North America Between France and England*, Brian Leigh Dunnigan, ed, Michael Cardy, trans. (New York: Old Fort Niagara Publishing, 1994), 259–262.
181. Webster, August 18, 1760, entry, 232–234.
182. Nathan Whiting, "Letters of Colonel Nathan Whiting, Written From Camp During the French and Indian War," Lemuel A. Welles, ed., in *Papers of the New Haven Colony Historical Society*, vol. 11 (New Haven, CT: published by the society, 1900), 145–147.
183. Whiting, 146.
184. William H. Guthman, *Drums A'beating, Trumpets Sounding: Artistically Carved Powder Horns in the Provincial Manner, 1746–1781* (Hartford: Connecticut Historical Society, 1993), 89–90, 129–131, 133–134, 138.
185. Malcomson, 17.
186. Webster, August 23, 1760, entry, 236–238.
187. Ibid., 236–238.
188. Ibid., August 25, 1760, entry, 239.
189. Ibid., August 26, 27, 28, 29, 30, 31, and September 1, 2, 3, 4, 1760, entries, 239–244.
190. Webster, September 4, 1760 entry, 244.
191. Rolls of Connecticut Men in the French and Indian War, vol. 10, 194–195.
192. Knox, 545, notes that Amherst reported to Pitt casualties in his land and naval forces of 26 killed and 42 wounded during the siege.
193. Webster, September 6, 1760 entry, 245.
194. Whiting, September 9 letter, 147–148.
195. Knox, 608, 612.
196. Webster, September 6, 1760, entry, 245.
197. Ibid., September 7, 1760, entry, 245.
198. Kemmer, 64–66.
199. Francis Parkman, *Montcalm and Wolfe* (New York: Barnes and Noble Books, 2005), 487.
200. Webster, September 7, 1760, entry, 245–246.
201. Knox, 589, footnote, notes that "most of the militia had before this abandoned the struggle."

202. Rolls of Connecticut Men in the French and Indian War , vol. 9 and 10. These names were gathered through exhaustive research of these records.
203. Webster, September 9, 10, 1760, entries, 247.
204. Ibid., September 10, 1760, entry, 247.
205. Rolls of Connecticut Men in the French and Indian War, vol. 10, 194–196.
206. Ibid., 237–283.
207. Chatham is presently called East Hampton.
208. Hoadley, vol. 13, 220. Timothy and Rowland Percival had their farms officially switched from the parish of Middle Haddam to the parish of East Hampton.
209. Public Land Records of East Hampton and East Haddam, vol. 3, 1–5, March 10, 1774. These documents reveal the transfer of land.
210. Brainard, 27, 30.

CHAPTER 5

211. Stephen Davies, http://web.via.ca/davies/H320/population.colonies.htm, accessed Feb. 23, 2010. Also, Albert E. Van Dusen, *Connecticut* (New York: Random House, 1961), 105; and Harold E. Selesky, *War and Society in Colonial Connecticut* (New Haven: Yale University Press, 1990), 70, 230.
212. Nathaniel Philbrick, *Mayflower* (New York: Penguin Books, 2006), 186. Philbrick states that "the average seventeenth-century New England house consumed fifteen cords, or 1,920 cubic feet of wood per year, meaning that a town of 200 homes depended on the deforestation of as many as seventy-five acres per year."
213. Ellis Sandoz, ed., *Political Sermons of the American Founding Era*, vol. 1 (1730–1788), 2nd ed. (Indianapolis, IN: Liberty Fund, 1998), xi, xii.
214. Hobart Estabrook, *The Praying Warrior, Mr. Estabrook's Sermon Preached May 30, 1758* (New Haven: James Parker & Co. 1758).
215. Carl F. Price, *Yankee Township* (East Hampton: Citizen's Welfare Club, 1941), 136.
Also, the son of Reverend John Norton served in the "Lexington Alarm " company from Chatham.
Henry P. Johnston, ed., *The Record of Connecticut Men in the Military and Naval Service During the War of the Revolution, 1775–1783* (Hartford, CT: Case, Lockwood, and Brainard Co., 1889), 6.
216. George S. Roberts, *Historic Towns of the Connecticut River Valley* (Schenectady, NY: Robson and Adee Publishers; digitized by the Arnold Bernhard Library, March 2005), 139–140.
217. Francis H. Parker, *Contributions to the History of East Haddam, Ct.* (Hartford: Connecticut State Library, 1938), 33, column 4.
218. Ibid., 34, column 2.
219. Price, 136.
220. Ibid., 136.
221. Henry P. Johnston, ed., *The Record of Connecticut Men in the Military and Naval Service During the War of the Revolution, 1775–1783* (Hartford, CT: Press of the Case, Lockwood, and Brainard Co., 1889), 6.

DANIEL D. KINLEY

222. Ibid., 5–28. The documents record forty-nine towns raising more than 3,800 men, some for a service of as little as one day, in response to the alarm from Lexington; the great majority marched to Boston, but some men also marched to New York.
223. Ibid., 6. Johnston records that most of the men were in service, and paid, for five days.
224. Ibid., 45–46.
225. Price, 136.
226. Johnston, 85–90.
227. Fitch, Jabez. "A Journal, from August 5th to December 13th, 1775. Kept by Lieutenant Jabez Fitch, Jr., of Norwich, of the 8th Company, Capt. Joseph Jewett's, in the Eighth Connecticut Regiment, Col. Jedidiah Huntington's, at the siege of Boston." *Proceedings of the Massachusetts Historical Society*, series 2, vol. 9, [Vol. 29 of continuous numbering] (Boston: published by the society, 1894–1895), 57, Sep. 15, 1775, entry.

I was able to ascertain which three companies from the Eighth Regiment were the last to arrive at Roxbury by listing all the regimental officers mentioned by Jabez Fitch in his journal between his arrival in August and September 30, 1775. It is logical to assume that a company was present if Fitch records any officer from that company. Through the process of elimination I found the three companies that arrived last.
228. Ibid., numerous entries, 40–62. All of the regiment's company commanders are mentioned in Fitch's journal before Sep. 30, 1775, except for the following: Maj. Clark's 3rd company, Capt. Lyon's 7th company, and Capt. Filer's 9th company (Percival's). On Sep. 30, 1775, Fitch mentions the arrival of Capt. Lyon. I assume the other two companies arrived the same day.
229. Ibid., 62, Sep. 29, 1775, entry.
230. Ibid., 51, September 1, 1775, entry.
231. Ibid., numerous entries refer to shortages.
232. Ibid., 64, Oct. 6, 1775, entry.
233. Francis S. Drake, *The Town of Roxbury* (facsimile reprint, Westminster, MD: Heritage Books, 1994; originally published, Roxbury, MA: by author, 1878), 46–47, 72, 76–80, 287, 372–374.
234. Ibid., 405, 414–415.
235. Samuel Bixby, "Diary of Samuel Bixby" and "Letters Illustrating the Siege," both in *Proceedings of the Massachusetts Historical Society*, vol. 14 (Boston: published by the society, 1876–1877), 285–298 and 275–285.
236. David McCullough, *1776* (New York: Simon and Schuster Paperbacks, 2005), 65.
237. Jedediah and Joshua Huntington, "Correspondence of the Brothers Joshua and Jedidiah Huntington During the Period of the American Revolution," in Huntington Papers, *Collections of the Connecticut Historical Society*, vol. 20 (Hartford: published by the society, 1923), 253.
238. Fitch, "A Journal, from August 5th to December 13th, 1775," 71, Oct. 21, 1775, entry.
239. Ibid., 71, Oct 22, 1775, entry.

COMMON COURAGE

240. Ibid., 72, Oct 24–26, 1775, entries.
241. http://www.connecticutsar.org/articles/scarlet_no2.htm, The Scarlet Standard, historical series, no. 2, August 1997.
242. Fitch, "A Journal, from August 5th to December 13th, 1775," 74–75, Oct 30, 1775, entry.
243. Ibid., 79, Nov. 12, 1775, entry.
244. Ibid., 80, Nov 14, 1755, entry.
245. Huntington, 254.
246. Ibid., 252–253.
247. Fitch, "A Journal, from August 5th to December 13th, 1775," 83, Nov 23, 1775, entry.
248. Ibid., 84, Nov. 24 entry; and 85, Nov 28, 1775, entry.
249. William Emerson, *Diaries and Letters of William Emerson, 1743–1776*, Amelia Forbes Emerson, ed. (Boston: Thomas Todd, 1972), 80.
250. Webb, 123, Dec. 1, 1775, letter.
251. Johnston, 89, 90.
252. McCullough, 30, 31.
253. W.B. Allen, ed., *George Washington, A Collection* (Indianapolis, IN: Liberty Fund, 1988), 55, Dec. 15, 1775, letter.
254. McCullough, 65.
255. Johnston, 102.
256. Huntington, 260.
257. Ibid., 265.
258. Johnston, 19, 107.
259. Huntington, 268.
260. "An Orderly Book From April 1775 to September 1775 during the Siege of Boston." *Proceedings of the Massachusetts Historical Society*, vol. 15 (Boston: published by the society, 1876–1877), 130.
261. James Thacher, MD, *Military Journal of the American Revolution, 1775–1783* (Gansevoort, NY: Corner House Historical Publications, 1998), 38.
262. Huntington, 269, Feb. 23, 1776, letter.
263. Thacher, 37–38.
264. Huntington, 271, Mar. 1, 1776, letter.
265. Samuel Blachley Webb, *Correspondence and Journals of Samuel Blachley Webb*, Worthington Chauncey Ford, ed. (Reprinted by Arno Press, 1969; originally published, New York and Lancaster, PA: Wickersham Press, 1893), 135.
266. McCullough, 105. Based on the number of naval vessels—three ships-of-line, plus frigates and other smaller vessels—these sailors and marines would also have been available for the defense of Boston.
267. Brendan Morrissey, *Boston 1775: The Shot Heard Around the World* (Oxford: Osprey Publishing, 1995), 77, note 1 to American Order of Battle.
268. McCullough, 89.
269. Ibid., 91.
270. Fitch, "Jabez Fitch Diary, January 4, 1776, to April 6, 1776." Transcribed by Carol and George Gadbois. Peter Force Collection, Manuscript Division, Library of Congress. 16, 17 (Mar. 4 entry).
271. Webb, 134.

DANIEL D. KINLEY

272. McCullough, 92.
273. Ibid., 38.
274. Ibid., 92.
275. Thacher, 38.
276. Fitch, "Jan. 4, 1776, to April 6, 1776," 17, Mar. 4 entry.
277. Thacher, 39.
278. McCullough, 94.
279. Ibid., 93.
280. Ibid., 94.
281. Thacher, 39.
282. McCullough, 93, lists twenty cannon in place during the siege of Boston, while Morrissey (55, American Order of Battle of June 17, 1775) lists only two four-pound cannon.
283. Thacher, 39–40.
284. McCullough, 96.
285. Fitch, "January 4, 1776, to April 6, 1776," 21, Mar. 17 entry.
286. McCullough, 107.

CHAPTER 6

287. Fitch, "January 4, 1776, to April 6, 1776;" 27.
288. McCullough, 115.
289. *Connecticut Courant*, April 22, 1776, number 587, at the Connecticut Historical Society, Hartford.
290. Jabez Huntington, "Correspondence of the Brothers Joshua and Jedediah Huntington during the Period of the American Revolution," In the Huntington Papers, *Collections of the Connecticut Historical Society*, vol. 20 (Hartford: published by the society, 1923), 278–279.
291. Ibid., 281–282.
292. Henry P. Johnston, *The Campaign of 1776 Around New York and Brooklyn* (Cranbury, NJ: Scholars Bookshelf, 2005; first published 1878), 35–37.
293. Ibid., 35–43.
294. Ibid., 70–91.
295. Ibid., 64.
296. Ibid., 79.
297. Ibid., 70–91.
298. Ibid., 92, footnote 1.
299. McCullough, 133.
300. Armand Francis Lucier, *Newspaper Datelines of the American Revolution*, vol. 3, May 1, 1776 to November 1, 1776 (Westminster, MD: Heritage Books, 2004), 109.
301. Bruce Bliven Jr., *Under the Guns* (New York: Harper and Row, 1972), 315.
302. Isaac Bangs, *Journal of Lieutenant Isaac Bangs, April 1 to July 29, 1776*, Edward Bangs, ed. In Eyewitness Accounts of the American Revolution series (n.p., Arno Press., 1968), 65.
303. Bangs, 54.
304. Bliven, 328.
305. Ibid., 329.

306. Huntington, 310.
307. Barnet Schechter, *The Battle for New York* (New York: Walker & Co., 2002), 102.
308. McCullough, 136–137.
309. Ibid., 137.
310. Johnston, *The Campaign of 1776 Around New York and Brooklyn*, 93, footnote 1.
311. Bangs, 58.
312. W. B. Allen, ed., *George Washington, A Collection* (Indianapolis, IN: Liberty Fund, 1988), 72.
313. McCullough, 131.
314. Johnston, *The Campaign of 1776 Around New York and Brooklyn*, 94.
315. McCullough, 150.
316. Connecticut Archives: Revolutionary War, series 1, 5, 273–274, July 24, 1776, includes note about David Moss.
317. Huntington, 321–322, August 19 and August 26, 1776, letters; also McCullough, 150–151.
318. Weather conditions taken from various diaries.
319. McCullough, 148.
320. Ibid., 129, states Americans had 120 cannon.
321. Johnston, *The Campaign of 1776 Around New York and Brooklyn*, 132, 133, notes 24,000 effective and 124–125 lists 28,500 American troops of which just under 20,000 were fit for duty.
322. McCullough, 148.
323. Ibid., 155–156.
324. Jabez Fitch, *The New-York Diary of Lieutenant Jabez Fitch of the 17th (Connecticut) Regiment From August 22, 1776 to December 15, 1776*, W.H. W. Sabine, ed. (New York: Colburn & Tegg, 1954), 25.
325. Huntington, 321–322.
326. Fitch, *The New-York Diary of Lieutenant Jabez Fitch of the 17th (Connecticut) Regiment From August 22, 1776 to December 15, 1776*, 25.
327. McCullough, 159.
328. Ibid., 153.
329. Fitch, *The New-York Diary of Lieutenant Jabez Fitch of the 17th (Connecticut) Regiment From August 22, 1776 to December 15, 1776*, 25–26.
330. Ibid., 26.
331. John J. Gallagher, *The Battle of Brooklyn 1776* (Edison: Castle Books, 1995) 93–94.
332. Fitch, *The New-York Diary of Lieutenant Jabez Fitch of the 17th (Connecticut) Regiment From August 22, 1776 to December 15, 1776*, 26–27.
333. Ibid., 27–28.
334. McCullough, 160, 161.
335. Fitch, 28.
336. Ibid.
337. Ibid., 30.
338. Johnston, *The Campaign of 1776 Around New York and Brooklyn*, 162–163.
339. McCullough, 169.
340. Schechter, 141, 142.

DANIEL D. KINLEY

341. Johnston, 162–163.
342. McCullough, 162.
343. There is some evidence from Fitch's journal, specifically from the letters of Colonel Huntington and other varied descriptions, that some members of the Seventeenth Continental Regiment actually had a uniform that was a brown or butternut-colored coat with black-colored facings. Yet, there are not enough conclusive sources to determine how many of the regiment were uniformed in this way.
344. Johnston, *The Campaign of 1776 Around New York and Brooklyn*, 33. The documents section has letters from General Parsons to John Adams describing the action.
345. Philip Katcher, *Uniforms of the Continental Army* (York, PA: George Shumway Publisher, 1981), 79, 89.
346. Johnston, *The Campaign of 1776 Around New York and Brooklyn*, 167.
347. McCullough, 171–172.
348. Johnston, *The Campaign of 1776 Around New York and Brooklyn*, 166–173, and accompanying map.
349. McCullough, 172.
350. Johnston, *The Campaign of 1776 Around New York and Brooklyn*, 168.
351. Johnston, *The Campaign of 1776 Around New York and Brooklyn*, documents section, 33–34.
352. Based on casualty report of the Seventeenth Regiment (Record of Service of Connecticut Men), 101–102, there were at least 200 officers and men in the regiment; divided into eight companies, there would be an average of 25 men per company.
353. Fitch, 87, note 1.
354. Mark Urban, *Fusiliers: The Saga of a British Redcoat Regiment in the American Revolution* (New York: Walker & Company, 2007), 83–84.
355. Ibid., 84, 85.
356. Johnston, *The Campaign of 1776 Around New York and Brooklyn*, 170–173.
357. Schecter, 146.
358. McCullough, 168–170.
359. Ibid., 176–178.
360. Gen. Parsons to John Adams, August 29, 1776, in Johnston, *The Campaign of 1776 Around New York and Brooklyn*, documents section, 33, 34.
361. Fitch, 30–31.
362. Gallagher, 117, 118.
363. Fitch, 31.
364. Record of Services of Connecticut Men in the War of the Revolution, 101–102.
365. Fitch, 31, and 33, footnote 9.
366. Ibid., 34.
367. Ibid., 34–35.
368. Ibid., 35–36, and "The Diary of Jabez Fitch, a Prison-Ship Martyr of 1776" (New York: William Abbatt, 1903), 139–140.
369. Ibid., 37, and "Prison-Ship Martyr," 140.
370. Ibid., 39–40, and "Prison-Ship Martyr," 142–143.
371. Ibid., 40.

COMMON COURAGE

372. Assumption based on casualty reports (Record of Service of Connecticut Men in the War of the Revolution, 101–102); with over 200 officers and men reported missing (captured), it's unlikely all the remaining 100 of Atlee's regiment would have escaped.
373. Fitch, 40–42.
374. Fitch, 42–54.
375. McCullough, 243.
376. Ibid., 240–244.
377. Fitch, "Prison-Ship Martyr," 148–149.
378. Fitch, 79, letter from Lieutenant Jonathan Gillet.
379. Fitch, 86–87.
380. Fitch, 104–105, 110.
381. Louise Hartley, "Mary Fuller Percival, a Humanitarian," *National Historical Magazine*, May 1941, 26–27.
382. Fitch, 230, 235.
383. Brendan Morrissey, *Saratoga 1777: Turning Point of a Revolution* (Oxford: Osprey Publishing, 2000), 86.
384. Fitch, 251.
385. Connecticut Archives: Revolutionary War, series 1, 12, 193–194. Percival is in Hartford May 28, 1778, to collect past wages.

EPILOGUE

386. Charles J. Hoadley, ed. *The Public Records of the State of Connecticut, From May, 1778, to April, 1780 Inclusive*, vol. 2 (Hartford: Press of the Case, Lockwood, and Brainard Co., 1880), 97.
387. Ibid., 101. Also, Rolls and Lists of Connecticut Men in the Revolution, 1775–1783, in *Collections of the Connecticut Historical Society*, vol. 3 (Hartford: published by the society, 1901), 221; and Henry P. Johnston, ed. *The Record of Connecticut Men in the Military and Naval Service During the War of the Revolution 1775–1783*, vols. 1–3 (Hartford: Case, Lockwood & Brainard Co.,1889), 614.
388. Henry J. Whittemore, *History of Middlesex County, Connecticut, with Special Sketches of its Prominent Men* (New York: J. B. Beers & Co., 1884), 503.
389. Louise Hartley, "Mary Fuller Percival, a Humanitarian," *National Historical Magazine*, May 1941, 26–27.
390. The town of Freehold was renamed Durham on March 28, 1805. Many of the early settlers came from Durham, CT, and called their settlement "New Durham." The name became popular and was finally adopted by universal consent as the appropriate name for the town.
391. 1790 census, Freehold, Albany County, NY, shows John Palmer as neighbor of Timothy Percival and lists Paul Percival there as well.
The 1810 census, Durham, Greene County, NY, shows Levi Stedman as neighbor of Timothy Percival, and lists Elkanah and Paul Percival there as well.
Homer W Brainard, *James Percival of Sandwich and Some of His Descendants* (Hartford, CT: n.p., 1925), 27, lists marriages of Mary and Anna Percival and move to Durham, NY.

DANIEL D. KINLEY

392. 1800 census, Freehold, NY, lists Elkanah Percival and Thomas, Moses, and Zerah Tousey. Brainard, 27: Timothy and Mary's daughter Lydia marries Thomas Tousey; 33: Paul's daughter Lydia marries Moses Tousey. On page 50, birthdates and locations of birth of children of Jabez Percival listed as Nov. 14, 1792, in Marlborough, MA; and Dec. 20, 1794, in Freehold, NY. Thus they moved sometime between those dates.
393. U.S. Census Bureau, http://www2.census.gov/prod2/decennial/documents/1820a-02.pdf, accessed April 9, 2010. Between the 1800 census and the 1820 census Connecticut's population grew about 10%, Delaware's about 12%, Massachusetts's about 24%, while areas bordering the Ohio River like Kentucky grew about 156%, and the Indiana Territory grew about 2820% (5,600 in 1800 to 147,000 in 1820).
394. *History of Dearborn and Ohio Counties, Indiana* (Chicago: F.E. Weakley & Co., 1885), 113–114, 165–167, 242.
395. Brainard, 33, mentions Lydia and George Whitman (children of Paul Percival) helping to start Touseytown, KY.
396. Jennifer S. Warner, *Boone County: From Mastodons to the Millennium* (Boone County Bicentennial Book Committee, 1998), 38.
397. Information supplied by Melinda Sartwell of Boone County, KY. Ms. Sartwell completed a research project for the Boone County Public Library in 2009 about the Percival family in Boone County, KY.
398. Boone County, KY, tax records, first record Timothy Percival in 1807.
399. 1810 census, Durham, NY, records Timothy Percival living there.
400. Hartley, 27.
401. Brainard, 27, records Timothy's and Mary's deaths in Boone County, KY. Boone County Will Book, A-237, August 19, 1815, provided by the Boone County Public Library, lists Timothy Percival's final accounting of belongings.

Boone County, KY, county court orders, 1799–1815, p. 291, July 3, 1815, mentions estate of Timothy Percival, Sr.
402. The War of the Austrian Succession, 1741–1748; The French and Indian War, 1755–1760; The War of Independence, 1775–1783; The War of 1812, 1812–1815.

CPSIA information can be obtained
at www.ICGtesting.com
Printed in the USA
LVIW012144200612
286973LV00008BB